B BLUE LABEL™
Inspired by you, powered by Best Buy®

You spoke. We listened.
Laptops with the features you asked for.

backlit keyboard

superior service & support

great portability

longer battery life

TOSHIBA
Leading Innovation >>>

optimal screen size

Satellite E105-S1402

Available exclusively at Best Buy
find out more at BestBuy.com / bluelabel

©2009 Best Buy

PERFECT GAME.

DESIGNATED HITTERS.

CAUGHT STEALING.

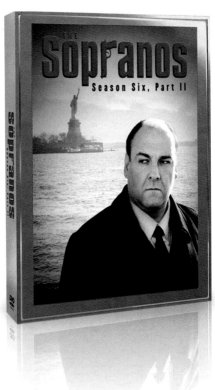

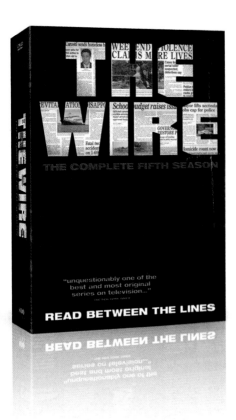

Own all of your favorite moments from all your favorite seasons.
Award-winning HBO® Original Series, now available on DVD.

AVAILABLE AT

1940 All-Star Game

12 Game Story
In St. Louis' first turn as host of the All-Star Game, a Missouri native stole the show in his first at-bat.

18 Local Angle
From the scene at the ballpark to the buzz around town, St. Louis' host-city role helped define the 1940 All-Star experience.

22 Major League Scene
Surveying All-Star subplots and story lines from around the majors.

26 The Season In Short
Charting the highs and lows of St. Louis' two big-league entries during their All-Star summer journeys.

1948 All-Star Game

32 Game Story   46 Major League Scene
40 Local Angle   52 The Season In Short

1957 All-Star Game

58 Game Story   74 Major League Scene
68 Local Angle   80 The Season In Short

1966 All-Star Game

86 Game Story   102 Major League Scene
96 Local Angle   108 The Season In Short

112 The Cardinals Constellation
A Cardinal-red galaxy of All-Star highlights since the inaugural Dream Game in 1933.

128 Cardinals All-Stars
Comprehensive season-by-season and all-time lists of the Cardinals' All-Star selections.

131 2009 Cardinals Player Gallery

4 Front-Office Directory
8 2009 Cardinals Schedule
188 Farm System Directory

The 2009 St. Louis Cardinals Yearbook is copyrighted by the St. Louis Cardinals L.L.C. **Publisher:** Steve Zesch **Editorial Associates:** Lauren Anderson, Katie Koss, Larry State **Photographers:** Dan Donovan, Bill Greenblatt, Jim Herren and Scott Rovak **Design:** Rock Wamsley **Production:** Jean Farrell **Advertising Sales:** Matt McSparin, (618) 406-2168 **For additional copies, contact:** St. Louis Cardinals Publications • 700 Clark St. • St. Louis, MO 63102 • Or call, 314-345-9303

Front Office

EXECUTIVE OFFICE

Chairman of the Board / General Partner	William O. DeWitt Jr.
Vice Chairman	Frederick O. Hanser
Senior Administrative Assistant	Grace Pak
Secretary-Treasurer	Andrew N. Baur
President	Bill DeWitt III
Senior Administrative Assistant	Julie Laningham
Vice President / General Manager	John Mozeliak
Executive Administrative Assistant to GM	Linda Brauer
Director, Government Affairs and Special Projects	Ron Watermon

BUSINESS OPERATIONS

SALES / BROADCASTING / PUBLICATIONS

Senior Vice President, Sales and Marketing	Dan Farrell
Administrative Assistant	Gail Ruhling

CORPORATE SALES

Vice President, Corporate Marketing and Stadium Entertainment	Thane van Breusegen
Director, Sales and Marketing Administration	Debbie Pfaff
Director, Scoreboard Operations and Senior Account Executive	Tony Simokaitis
Cardinals Productions	Craig Wilson
Senior Corporate Sales Account Executive	Jeff Floerke
Corporate Sales Account Executive	Joe Pfeiffer
Account Coordinator / Manager of Promotions	Kristin Casey
Corporate Sales Account Services	Katie Bassel, Kyra Joiner, Scott Stevens
Corporate Sales Coordinator	Kristin Sneller
Radio Sales Account Executives	Kyle Dinges, Chris Turley, Craig Unger
Coordinator, Cardinals Radio Network	Anne Carroll

TICKET SALES

Vice President, Ticket Sales	Joe Strohm
Administrative Assistant	Lisa Haffer
Manager, Ticket Technology	Jennifer Needham
Receptionist	Marilyn Mathews
Direct Sales Representatives	Drew Brucker, Beth Dean, Jama Fabry, Amy Oakes, Matt Papes, Brittany Rowan, Michael Salony, David Sowa, Tia Washington, Matt Willett

FAN DEVELOPMENT / ALUMNI RELATIONS

Director, Fan Development and Alumni Relations	Martin Coco
Supervisor, Fan Development	Melissa Tull
Coordinator, Fan Development	Taylor Pope
Coordinator, Ticket Sales	Molly Radcliffe

GROUP SALES

Manager, Small Groups	Mary Clare Bena
Account Executives, Group Sales	Raley Curry, Laura Elliott
Manager, Large Groups	Kristi Yehling
Senior Account Executive, Group Sales	Linda Burnside
Account Executives, Group Sales	Mollie Francis, Matt Kitchell, Don Loughridge, Kevin Mueller, Gina Perschbacher, Stephanie Roth, Cullen Speckhals

PREMIUM TICKET SALES

Manager, Premium Ticket Sales	Dolores Scanlon
Supervisor, Premium Ticket Sales	Julie Nienhuis

SEASON TICKET SALES AND SERVICE

Manager, Season Ticket Sales and Service	Jamie Brickler
Account Executives, Season Ticket Service	Kim Bussen, Ryan Eberhart, Mike Lucchesi, Justen Meyer, Brett Reitz, Emmalee Steiger

TICKET SERVICES

Director, Ticket Services	Derek Throneburg
Manager, Ticket Services	Brady Bruhn
Coordinator, Ticket Services	Heather Bacon
Ticket Service Representatives	Diana Auer, Pat Brewer, Jolene Jungers, Nancy Landa, Paul Pohlman, Andrea Robinson

PUBLICATIONS

Director, Publications	Steve Zesch
Publications Staff	Lauren Anderson, Katie Koss, Larry State

COMMUNITY RELATIONS

Vice President, Cardinals Care and Community Relations	Michael Hall
Administrative Assistant	Mary Ellen Edmiston
Coordinator, Cardinals Care	Lucretia Payne
Community Relations Communications Specialist	Mark Taylor
Cardinals Care Youth Baseball Commissioner	Keith Brooks
Cardinals Care / Community Relations Supervisor	Jessica Illert
Director, Target Marketing	Ted Savage

FINANCE

Senior Vice President and Chief Financial Officer	Brad Wood
Administrative Assistant	Marcia Moore
Director, Finance	Rex Carter
Director, Purchasing and Cost Analysis	Mark Murray
Manager, Accounting	John Lowry
Manager, Payroll and Compliance Reporting	Shellie Stephens
Supervisor, Ticket Accounting and Reporting	Michelle Flach
Payroll Accountants	Lurena Frenchie, Lee Weber
Senior Accountant	Tracey Sessions
Accountants	Patty Cooper, Kurt Hoevel, Bernie Steele

Building on a tradition of excellence in our hometown.

As a Cards fan, you'd go to the ends of the earth to support your team. Fortunately, you don't have to go that far for your family's health. From season to season, Gateway Regional Medical Center's skilled physicians and caring staff work tirelessly to make sure everybody is a fan of ours. Expect great things from your hometown team and your hometown hospital.

 GATEWAY REGIONAL MEDICAL CENTER

2100 Madison Avenue, Granite City, IL 62040
www.gatewayregional.net

Front Office

DIRECTORY

Accounting Assistant	Marissa Hoover
Office Services Coordinator	Bernie Fassler
Auditor	Grace McGowan

STADIUM OPERATIONS

Vice President, Stadium Operations	Joe Abernathy
Director, Stadium Operations	Mike Bertani
Director, Security and Special Services	Joe Walsh
Director, Quality Assurance and Guest Services	Mike Ball
Manager, Stadium Operations and Guest Services Quality Assurance	Cindy Richards
Stadium Operations Assistant	Ashleigh Middlebrook
Stadium Operations Systems Administrator	Hosei Maruyama
Stadium Operations Administrative Assistant and Safety Coordinator	Hope Baker
Shipping and Receiving Assistant	Joe Humphries
Housekeeping Supervisor	Scott Jackson
Head Groundskeeper	Bill Findley
Assistant Head Groundskeeper	Chad Casella
Stadium Operations General Labor Crew	Renay Ellis, Terry Moll
Mechanical Technicians	Ken Biekert, Kyle Creamer, Sean Driver
Mechanic	Gene Ross
Carpenter	Barry Abbett
Painter	Bill Martin

EVENT SERVICES

Vice President, Event Services & Merchandising	Vicki Bryant
Administrative Assistant	Barb Amrich
Manager, Special Events	Kevin Owen
Administrative Assistant	Kristen Schmalz
Manager, Event Services	Missy Tobey
Manager, Retail Operations	Pat Daly

HALL OF FAME MUSEUM

Manager, Museum Operations and Curator	Paula Homan
Manager, Stadium Tours and Museum Outreach	Brian Finch
Registrar	Jennifer Jackson

HUMAN RESOURCES

Director, Human Resources	Christine Nelson
Administrative Assistant	Celina Allen
Benefits Manager	Karen Brown

BASEBALL OPERATIONS
MANAGER / COACHES / SUPPORT STAFF

Field Manager	Tony La Russa
Pitching Coach	Dave Duncan
Batting Coach	Hal McRae
First-Base Coach	Dave McKay
Third-Base Coach	Jose Oquendo
Bench Coach	Joe Pettini
Bullpen Coach	Marty Mason
Assistant Batting Coach	Mike Aldrete
Special Assistant to the General Manager	Red Schoendienst
Major League Trainer	Barry Weinberg
Assistant Major League Trainer	Greg Hauck
Strength and Conditioning Coach	Pete Prinzi
Equipment Manager	Rip Rowan
Assistant Equipment Manager	Ernie Moore
Visiting Clubhouse Manager	Jerry Risch
Traveling Secretary	C.J. Cherre
Video Coordinator, Major Leagues	Chad Blair

PLAYER DEVELOPMENT / SCOUTING

Vice President, Amateur Scouting / Player Development	Jeff Luhnow
Assistant General Manager	John Abbamondi
Administrative Assistant	Ellen Gingles
Special Assistants to the General Manager	Mike Jorgensen, Gary LaRocque, Matt Slater
Director of Major League Administration	Judy Carpenter-Barada
Director, Minor League Operations	John Vuch
Director, Baseball Development	Mike Girsch
Coordinator, Asian Development	Rob Fidler
Senior Quantitative Analyst	Sig Mejdal
Assistant Director of Scouting	Jaron Madison
Coordinator, Pro Scouting	Matt Carroll
Professional Scouts	Bruce Benedict, Alan Benes, Chuck Fick, Mike Jorgensen, Marty Keough, Gary LaRocque, Deric McKamey, Joe Rigoli, Matt Slater
National/Regional Supervisors	Joe Almaraz, Mike Roberts, Roger Smith
Area Scouts	Matt Blood, Jay Catalano, Mike Elias, Ralph Garr Jr., Charlie Gonzalez, Brian Hopkins, Jeff Ishii, Mike Juhl, Aaron Krawiec, Aaron Looper, Scott Melvin, Sean Moran, Jamal Strong, Matt Swanson
Director, International Operations	Moises Rodriguez
Latin American Supervisor	Juan Mercado
International Scouts	Crysthiam Blanco (Nicaragua), Fermin Colonel (Dutch Antilles), Domingo Garcia (Dominican Republic), Jose Gregoria Gonzalez (Venezuela), Carlos Heron (Panama), Neder Horta (Colombia), Carlos Lugo (Dominican Republic), Rene Rojas (Dominican Republic)

MEDIA RELATIONS

Director, Media Relations	Brian Bartow
Assistant Directors, Media Relations	Jim Anderson, Melody Yount
Media Relations Assistant	Jared Odom

1929: Twenty minutes from Sportsman's Park

2009: Eight minutes from Busch Stadium
and all the Gateway Arch Riverfront activites

(618) 337-6060
www.stlouisdowntownairport.com

Game Schedule

2009

APRIL

SUN	MON	TUE	WED	THU	FRI	SAT
			1	2	3	4
5	6 FS PIT 3:15	7 FS PIT 7:15	8 FS PIT 7:15	9 FS PIT 12:40	10 FS HOU 7:15	11 F HOU 3:10
12 K HOU 1:15	13 FS ARI 8:40	14 FS ARI 8:40	15 FS ARI 2:40	16 FS CHI 1:20	17 FS CHI 1:20	18 F CHI 2:40
19 E CHI PPD	20	21 FS NY 7:15	22 FS NY 7:15	23 FS NY 12:40	24 FS CHI 7:15	25 F CHI 3:10
26 K CHI 1:15	27 FS ATL 6:10	28 FS ATL 6:10	29 FS ATL 6:10	30 FS WSH 6:05		

MAY

SUN	MON	TUE	WED	THU	FRI	SAT
					1 FS WSH 6:05	2 FS WSH 12:05
3 K WSH PPD	4 FS PHI 7:15	5 FS PHI 7:15	6 FS PHI 7:15	7 FS PHI 12:40	8 FS CIN 6:10	9 FS CIN 6:10
10 K CIN 12:10	11	12 FS PIT 6:05	13 FS PIT 6:05	14 FS PIT 6:05	15 FS MIL PPD	16 FS MIL 12:10
17 K MIL 1:15	18 FS MIL 7:15	19 FS CHI 7:15	20 FS CHI 7:15	21 FS CHI 7:15	22 FS KC 7:15	23 FS KC 12:10
24 K KC 1:15	25 FS MIL 1:05	26 FS MIL 7:05	27 FS MIL 12:05	28	29 FS SF 9:15	30 FS SF 8:05
31 K SF 3:05						

JUNE

SUN	MON	TUE	WED	THU	FRI	SAT
	1 FS CIN 7:15	2 FS CIN 7:15	3 FS CIN 7:15	4 FS CIN 7:15	5 FS COL 7:15	6 FS COL 6:15
7 K COL 1:15	8 FS COL 1:15	9 FS FLA 6:10	10 FS FLA 6:10	11 FS FLA 11:10	12 FS CLE 6:05	13 F CLE 3:05
14 E CLE 7:05	15	16 FS DET 7:15	17 FS DET 7:15	18 FS DET 7:15	19 FS KC 7:10	20 F KC 3:10
21 FS KC 1:10	22 FS NY 6:10	23 FS NY 6:10	24 FS NY 6:10	25 FS NY 12:10	26 FS MIN 7:15	27 FS MIN 12:10
28 K MIN 1:15	29 FS SF 1:15	30 FS SF 1:15				

JULY

SUN	MON	TUE	WED	THU	FRI	SAT
			1 FS SF 7:15	2 FS SF 6:15	3 FS CIN 6:10	4 FS CIN 12:10
5 FS CIN 12:10	6	7 FS MIL 7:05	8 FS MIL 7:05	9 FS MIL 1:05	10 FS CHI 1:20	11 F CHI 3:10
12 CHI K 12:05 E 7:05	13	14 (All-Star Game)	15	16	17 FS ARI 7:15	18 FS ARI 6:15
19 FS ARI 1:15	20 FS HOU 7:05	21 FS HOU 7:05	22 FS HOU 7:05	23 FS WSH 6:05	24 FS PHI 6:05	25 F PHI 3:05
26 K PHI 12:35	27 FS LA 7:15	28 FS LA 7:15	29 FS LA 7:15	30 FS LA 7:15	31 FS HOU 7:15	

AUGUST

SUN	MON	TUE	WED	THU	FRI	SAT
						1 FS HOU 6:15
2 K HOU 1:15	3	4 FS NY 6:10	5 FS NY 11:10	6	7 FS PIT 6:05	8 FS PIT 6:05
9 K PIT 12:35	10 FS CIN 7:15	11 FS CIN 7:15	12 FS CIN 7:15	13	14 FS SD 7:15	15 FS SD 6:15
16 K SD 1:15	17 FS LA 9:10	18 FS LA 9:10	19 FS LA 9:10	20 FS SD 9:05	21 FS SD 9:05	22 FS SD 9:05
23 K SD 3:05	24	25 FS HOU 7:15	26 FS HOU 7:15	27 FS HOU 1:15	28 FS WSH 7:15	29 FS WSH 7:15
30 K WSH 1:15	31					

SEPT./OCT.

SUN	MON	TUE	WED	THU	FRI	SAT
		1 FS MIL 7:15	2 FS MIL 7:15	3 FS MIL 1:15	4 FS PIT 6:05	5 FS PIT 6:05
6 FS PIT 12:35	7 FS MIL 1:05	8 FS MIL 7:05	9 FS MIL 1:05	10	11 FS ATL 7:15	12 F ATL 3:10
13 ATL 1:15	14 FS FLA 7:15	15 FS FLA 7:15	16 FS FLA 1:15	17	18 FS CHI 7:15	19 FS CHI 3:10
20 CHI 1:15	21 FS HOU 7:05	22 FS HOU 7:05	23 FS HOU 7:05	24	25 FS COL 7:10	26 FS COL 7:10
27 K COL 2:10	28	29 FS CIN 6:10	30 FS CIN 6:10	1 FS CIN 11:35	2 FS MIL 7:15	3 K MIL 12:10
4 K MIL 1:15						

HOME AWAY

All games on 550 KTRS Radio
FS: FS Midwest   F: FOX
K: KSDK Channel 5   E: ESPN

Dates, times and TV networks are subject to change

Gives "Ballpark Dog" a whole new meaning.

PURINA *Pooches* IN THE BALLPARK

See you and your dog at the ballpark!

Visit Purina.com for details.

PURINA®
Your Pet, Our Passion.®

★ 1940 ALL-STAR GAME ★

NATIONAL LEAGUE 4, AMERICAN LEAGUE 0

SPORTSMAN'S PARK, JULY 9

OFFICIAL PROGRAM

MAJOR LEAGUE ALL STAR GAME

SPORTSMAN'S PARK SAINT LOUIS   Price 25 Cents   TUESDAY JULY 9, 1940 1:30 P.M.

Conformity wasn't part of the strategy of All-Star managers Bill McKechnie (left) of Cincinnati and Joe Cronin of the Red Sox.

St. Louis was at the center of the baseball universe on July 9, 1940, when the major leagues' top stars aligned at Sportsman's Park for the eighth Midsummer Classic. Playing host to the All-Star Game for the first time was heady stuff for St. Louisans, all of whom wanted the representatives of their city's two big-league teams – two Cardinals and one member of the Browns – to show off their wares and ignite some civic pride. Most of them also hoped the National League would spank an American League squad dominated by New York Yankees.

Seven Yanks had been listed on the Americans' roster when the makeup of the team was announced, and in many fans' eyes, the New York franchise already was entrenched as baseball's Evil Empire. Even supporters of the A.L.'s lowly Browns couldn't muster much rooting interest in the American League All-Stars – not when their Brownies were routinely being pummeled in regular-season play by the big-spending, ridiculously successful evildoers from the Bronx.

Provincialism was not rewarded on this steamy 90-degree afternoon – unless, that is, you tweak the typical immediacy of its boundaries – but anti-Yankees sentiment did have its day, as the National League dealt the A.L. the first shutout loss in All-Star history, 4-0.

The game lacked drama but not the unexpected. Under the format in place at the time, the A.L. and N.L. managers were responsible for picking their starting lineups after 25-man rosters had been chosen by a vote of all eight managers in each league.

The American League anointed the Red Sox's Joe Cronin to guide its All-Stars, in a move that went against tradition. (The previous year's World Series manager typically got the assignment, and Boston had finished second to New York in 1939.) The decision to relieve the Yanks' Joe McCarthy of A.L. managerial duties seemed to be tacit admission that fans

everywhere were weary of the Yankees, who had throttled the N.L. champions in the previous four World Series.

Yet Cronin named the Yankees' Red Ruffing – who had a middling 7-6 record – his starting pitcher. Head-scratching over the move was nearly audible, considering Detroit's Bobo

(From left) Starting pitchers Red Ruffing (A.L.) and Paul Derringer (N.L.) decided their clubs' respective fates.

★ 1940 ALL-STAR GAME ★

In the first, and only, All-Star at-bat of his career, Max West ensured his everlasting place in Dream Game lore.

Newsom and Cleveland's Bob Feller and Al Milnar had a combined 36-9 record at the All-Star break.

The puzzling choice to start Ruffing was matched by a surprising lineup decision by Bill McKechnie. The National League manager opted to play Max West of the Boston Bees in right field ahead of New York Giants slugger Mel Ott, who had been considered a cinch to start. McKechnie's managerial acumen proved divine; Cronin's abysmal.

Cincinnati's pilot at the time, McKechnie boasted a long and impressive resume that included leading the Cardinals to the pennant in 1928. He picked Reds ace Paul Derringer to start the game, and Derringer – who also had started against Ruffing in the 1939 All-Star Game – pitched hitless ball in the top of the first.

Pittsburgh's Arky Vaughan greeted Ruffing with a bad-hop single to begin the bottom half of the inning, and the Cubs' Billy Herman followed with a hit-and-run single that sent Vaughan scurrying to third. Up stepped West, a Missouri native who at age 23 was in his third major league season.

Ruffing surely was glad to see West – not Ott – in the batter's box, even though Max entered the game with a .285 batting average compared with Ott's .277. West had batted only .234 with 10 home runs in his rookie season of 1938 before improving to a .285 average and 19 homers in 1939. Ott was recognized as one of the game's great power hitters – he was sitting on 375 career home runs at the time – and he had hit six homers to West's three at that point of the 1940 season.

No matter. West drove a one-strike pitch into the right-field pavilion. It was N.L. 3, A.L. 0 before Ruffing had retired a batter.

The usually fun-loving Newsom no doubt was seething as he watched the proceedings. "Here I am with a 12-and-1 record and they give me the runaround," Newsom had cracked the night before. "Buck starts, or he doesn't pitch at all. To hell with the All-Stars." To the surprise of no one, Buck was blowing smoke; he took over for Ruffing in the fourth inning.

Oddly, West's presence in the starting lineup was based on McKechnie's defensive strategy. The N.L. manager wanted to solidify the defense by using Ott in the late innings, when right field would be the sun field.

"It was my hunch that Ott, who is older (31) and more experienced, would be a bit steadier in the sun, and that is the only reason for the change," McKechnie explained after the game.

In becoming the first player to hit a home run in his first All-Star at-bat, West provided a touch of home-state pride for the crowd of 32,373, although Max's ties to the area were tenuous. Born in Dexter, a town situated 170 miles south of St. Louis, West moved to California at a young age.

Still, the displaced Missourian gave St. Louis fans more to cheer about than the performances of their own big-league representatives. Cardinals first baseman Johnny Mize and center fielder Terry Moore, both starters, went a combined 0-for-5 at the plate; Browns first baseman George McQuinn, who was hobbled with a leg injury, was projected for possible reserve duty but never got off the pine.

West couldn't quite grasp all the excitement over his big moment. "That's why I was up there at the plate – to hit that ball – wasn't it?" he asked, adding that he had "never seen such a swell pitch for a batter to hit in our National League."

Queried about Ruffing's gopher ball, West said, "Gee, I don't know what he threw. It just looked like a good one to hit." Ruffing's take: "It was a low fastball, but it sure seemed faster after he swung."

West's home run earned the low-profile Boston player his 15 minutes of fame, but Max wasn't able to enjoy the moment for even that long. While chasing a second-inning drive by Luke Appling that went for a double, West crashed into the right-field wall and crumpled to the ground. His left hip badly bruised, West left the game and was replaced by the Cubs' Bill Nicholson.

The Nationals – blanked by Newsom over the middle three

innings – didn't score again until the eighth, when Ott drew a leadoff walk against Feller, advanced to second on a bunt and scored on a single by the Giants' Harry Danning, the N.L.'s leading hitter at .343 and top RBI man with 58.

Of course, the N.L. All-Stars didn't need to score again against Cronin's crew, not with Derringer, Reds teammate Bucky Walters, the Dodgers' Whitlow Wyatt, the Cubs' Larry French and the Giants' Carl Hubbell combining for the whitewash. They allowed

West's moment in the sun was short-lived. A half-inning after his homer put the National League up 3-0, he hobbled off the All-Star stage after crashing into the concrete right-field wall at Sportsman's Park.

★ 1940 ALL-STAR GAME ★

three hits overall – two by the White Sox's Appling and the other by that Newsom fellow – with only Appling reaching second base. With not much going on for the A.L., the Nationals took care of business in a snappy 1 hour, 53 minutes, still an All-Star record for brevity.

Cronin's handling of the A.L. roster drew considerable criticism, and it wasn't limited to his decision to start Ruffing (a move he defended by saying he had expected Ruffing's half-speed stuff to fool N.L. hitters, setting the table for Newsom and Feller to overwhelm them with their hardball offerings).

When McCarthy started five of his Yankees in the 1937 classic and six Bronx Bombers in the 1939 game – both American League victories – no one questioned him. After all, his '37 and '39 New York juggernauts entered the breaks with 44-22 and 53-22 records, and those Yankee teams were on the way to A.L. pennants and decisive World Series triumphs.

But when Cronin opted to start five members of the pinstriped set in the 1940 All-Star Game, there were howls. The Yankees were 37-34 and residing in fourth place, yet Cronin's opening lineup listed Joe DiMaggio in center field, Charlie Keller in right, Joe Gordon at second base, Bill Dickey behind the plate and Ruffing on the mound. DiMaggio and Keller had been playing well, but Gordon was struggling with a .245 average and Dickey was hitting a puny .221. In his last start before the break, Ruffing had yielded seven hits, five runs and five walks in a four-inning stint against the lowly Athletics.

Frederick G. Lieb, noted baseball historian and scribe, wrote in *The Sporting News* that Cronin "managed his club as though he still were hypnotized by the glamour of the Yankees.... For several years, especially in the All-Star Game in Washington (an 8-3 A.L. romp in '37), the great McCarthy players rode roughshod over National League opponents, just as they had done in World's Series play. Their praises were sung to the skies. Therefore, it is no more than fair to say that the failure of the 1940 American League team was due in large measure to the shortcomings of these same Yankees."

Just how short did Yankees players come up in this game? Ruffing, of course, put the Americans in a sizable hole, and he yielded five hits overall in three innings. Then, as the A.L. squad attempted to rebound from its early deficit, the Americans' offense got absolutely nothing – as in 0-for-9 – from New York's position players.

On the other hand, McKechnie won praise for his deft and liberal use of the roster. At a time when the N.L. was coping with an inferiority complex – it had lost five of the first seven All-Star Games and 10 of the past 13 World Series – no one would have blamed McKechnie if he had taken a McCarthyesque approach to winning the game. (McCarthy had played his position players all the way in the 1937 and 1939 classics.)

But McKechnie dared to remove five of his starting position players – plus Nicholson, who had replaced West – in the top of the sixth. Having taken out starting catcher Ernie Lombardi (Reds) earlier, McKechnie wound up using 22 of his 25 players.

Only one National Leaguer – the Cardinals' Moore – played the entire game, and it wasn't out of deference to St. Louis fans. The center fielder was employed throughout because of his considerable defensive skills, coupled with his familiarity with the nooks and crannies of Sportsman's Park.

The N.L. manager made several other shrewd moves. He felt no qualms about using his Cincinnati standouts, Derringer and Walters, to lead off the game, and they pitched one-hit ball over four innings. McKechnie went against the established three-inning workload for All-Star pitchers, getting maximum efficiency by using four hurlers for two innings each. He started Herman at second, and reaped the benefits of the infielder's 3-for-3 performance. He employed Danning as the Nationals' third catcher of the day, and Harry the Horse knocked in the final N.L. run. And Deacon Bill had just the man to trot out as the ultimate closer – the screwballing Hubbell, then 37 years old and six years removed from his All-Star feat of striking out five consecutive future Hall of Famers. King Carl fanned the first batter he faced, Cleveland's Ken Keltner, in a hitless ninth.

Oh yes, McKechnie also played a big-time hunch, otherwise known as a masterstroke: He penciled in Max West as his starting right fielder.

Joe Hoppel is a free-lance writer based in St. Louis.

Cubs second baseman Billy Herman had as many hits as the American League team, posting a 3-for-3 afternoon with a run scored.

Sportsman's Park

N.L. 4, A.L. 0

American League	AB	R	H	RBI	BB	SO
Cecil Travis (Senators) 3B	3	0	0	0	0	0
Ken Keltner (Indians) 3B	1	0	0	0	0	1
Ted Williams (Red Sox) LF	2	0	0	0	1	0
Lou Finney (Red Sox) RF	0	0	0	0	1	0
Charlie Keller (Yankees) RF	2	0	0	0	0	1
Hank Greenberg (Tigers) LF	2	0	0	0	0	0
Joe DiMaggio (Yankees) CF	4	0	0	0	0	0
Jimmie Foxx (Red Sox) 1B	3	0	0	0	0	1
Luke Appling (White Sox) SS	3	0	2	0	0	0
Lou Boudreau (Indians) SS	0	0	0	0	0	0
Bill Dickey (Yankees) C	1	0	0	0	0	0
Frank Hayes (Athletics) C	1	0	0	0	0	0
Rollie Hemsley (Indians) C	1	0	0	0	0	0
Joe Gordon (Yankees) 2B	2	0	0	0	0	2
a-Ray Mack (Indians) PH-2B	1	0	0	0	0	1
Red Ruffing (Yankees) P	1	0	0	0	0	0
Bobo Newsom (Tigers) P	1	0	1	0	0	0
Bob Feller (Indians) P	1	0	0	0	0	1
Totals	**29**	**0**	**3**	**0**	**2**	**7**

National League	AB	R	H	RBI	BB	SO
Arky Vaughan (Pirates) SS	3	1	1	0	0	1
Eddie Miller (Braves) SS	1	0	0	0	0	1
Billy Herman (Cubs) 2B	3	1	3	0	0	0
Pete Coscarart (Dodgers) 2B	1	0	0	0	0	1
Max West (Braves) RF	1	1	1	3	0	0
Bill Nicholson (Cubs) RF	2	0	0	0	0	0
Mel Ott (Giants) RF	0	1	0	0	1	0
Johnny Mize (Cardinals) 1B	2	0	0	0	0	0
Frank McCormick (Reds) 1B	1	0	0	0	0	0
Ernie Lombardi (Reds) C	2	0	1	0	0	0
Babe Phelps (Dodgers) C	0	0	0	0	1	0
Harry Danning (Giants) C	1	0	1	1	0	0
Joe Medwick (Dodgers) LF	2	0	0	0	0	0
Jo-Jo Moore (Giants) LF	2	0	0	0	0	0
Cookie Lavagetto (Dodgers) 3B	2	0	0	0	0	0
Pinky May (Phillies) 3B	1	0	0	0	0	0
Terry Moore (Cardinals) CF	3	0	0	0	1	1
Paul Derringer (Reds) P	1	0	0	0	0	1
Bucky Walters (Reds) P	0	0	0	0	0	0
Whitlow Wyatt (Dodgers) P	1	0	0	0	0	1
Larry French (Cubs) P	0	0	0	0	0	0
Carl Hubbell (Giants) P	0	0	0	0	0	0
Totals	**29**	**4**	**7**	**4**	**3**	**6**

												R	H	E
American League	0	0	0	0	0	0	0	0	0	–		0	3	1
National League	3	0	0	0	0	0	0	1	X	–		4	7	0

American League	IP	H	R	ER	BB	SO	HR	BF
Red Ruffing (Yankees) L	3	5	3	3	0	2	1	14
Bobo Newsom (Tigers)	3	1	0	0	1	1	0	11
Bob Feller (Indians)	2	1	1	1	2	3	0	10
Totals	**8**	**7**	**4**	**4**	**3**	**6**	**1**	**35**

National League	IP	H	R	ER	BB	SO	HR	BF
Paul Derringer (Reds) W	2	1	0	0	1	3	0	8
Bucky Walters (Reds)	2	0	0	0	0	0	0	6
Whitlow Wyatt (Dodgers)	2	1	0	0	0	1	0	6
Larry French (Cubs)	2	1	0	0	0	2	0	7
Carl Hubbell (Giants)	1	0	0	0	1	1	0	4
Totals	**9**	**3**	**0**	**0**	**2**	**7**	**0**	**31**

a-Struck out for Gordon in eighth. E: Hemsley. DP: NL, Coscarart-Miller-McCormick. LOB: American 4, National 7. 2B: Appling. HR: West. SH: McCormick, French. HBP: May. Umpires: HP - Beans Reardon, 1B - George Pipgras, 2B - Bill Stewart, 3B - Steve Basil. Time: 1:53. Attendance: 32,373.

Batting seventh...

The 1940 All-Star Game had been officially awarded to St. Louis a year earlier – with the Cardinals designated as hosts – during owners meetings held in conjunction with the All-Star gala at Yankee Stadium. Of the majors' 10 metropolitan locales – which included two teams in four cities and three clubs in New York – St. Louis became the seventh to host the event.

The Dream Game was the brainchild of *Chicago Tribune* sports editor Arch Ward, who in 1933 conceived the American League-National League showdown as a feature attraction for Chicago's Century of Progress Exposition, the city's World's Fair.

For the 1940 edition of the game, the Chase Hotel served as headquarters for the American Leaguers, while the National League staff and players settled in at the Hotel Jefferson.

Resident All-Stars

The gala's fledgling history included only seven games at this juncture, but the selection of All-Star teams already was stirring annual debate over who belonged and who didn't. Local fans voiced one major complaint over the 1940 picks: the absence of Browns outfielder Rip Radcliff from the American League squad.

On the day rosters were disclosed, Radcliff was the A.L.'s leading hitter; when the Americans took the field on July 9, he was at .355 and second only to Boston's Lou Finney in the league batting race.

St. Louis had to settle for placing only three representatives on the All-Star rosters – the Browns' George McQuinn, an A.L. reserve, and the Cardinals' Johnny Mize and Terry Moore, both N.L. starters. There was, however, a third Cardinal on the field at Sportsman's Park: righthander Lon Warneke. Like many Cardinals, Warneke had endured a tough first half of the season; he was serving as one of the N.L. batting-practice pitchers.

Pepper Martin, whose failure to land an All-Star spot was derided in some quarters, was on hand for the game as a spectator. The Cards' firebrand was in his usual casual attire – no tie, no coat – and chomping on popcorn.

Hardheaded scorn

The possibility that protective headgear might soon be worn in the majors – the innovation had just won approval by the N.L. as beanball wars mounted – was a hot topic in St. Louis, as photographers tried to get candid shots of players in the still-to-be-perfected helmets. The catch: Few players would cooperate; it was as if the "don't call me a sissy club" had been called to order.

"I wouldn't let one of my players wear it, not even for a picture," hissed Pirates manager Frankie Frisch, an All-Star

From the scene at the ballpark to the buzz around town, St. Louis' host-city role helped define the 1940 All-Star experience.

Terry Moore gave the home crowd a permanent rooting interest as the only N.L. All-Star to play all nine innings.

spectator. Another former Gas Houser, Dodgers playing manager Leo Durocher, chipped in: "I haven't been hit in 10 years, and I'm not going to make myself a target now."

The Cards' Moore at least agreed to pose in a helmet. "They might be all right if they get a good one," allowed the center fielder, who then added: "But I'll never wear one."

Redbirds skipper Billy Southworth said helmets had been tried in the International League but proved unsuccessful, and he didn't think they'd be accepted in the big leagues, either.

Drawing a crowd

The Sportsman's Park gates were supposed to open at 8 a.m. – the first pitch was scheduled for 1:30 p.m. – but there was a half-hour delay in cranking loose the turnstiles.

The *St. Louis Star-Times* took note of an early-arriving crowd, reporting that "two lines of shirt-sleeved men laughed and joked for many hours" before the gates finally opened. The newspaper said some bleacherites were nursing sore backs, the result of catching naps on the pavement as they awaited the big game. By 10 a.m., the bleachers were about one-third full.

The official crowd for the day numbered 32,373 – a figure that thrilled Cardinals owner Sam Breadon, who boasted that "this little town" had outdrawn three previous All-Star hosts: Boston, Washington and Cincinnati.

Despite a few empty seats in the center-field bleachers, Breadon – in the view of *Star-Times* sports editor Sid Keener – saw the game as re-establishing St. Louis' standing as a baseball town. (Cardinals season attendance had plunged below 300,000 two years earlier, and the Browns' gate, incredibly, had dipped below the 100,000 mark three times in the 1930s.)

All-Star Game ticket demand turned into a profitable business – briefly – for two New York men, who were scalping $1.42 ducats for $3.85 out of an East St. Louis hotel until they were nabbed by the city's finest.

The game's primary beneficiary, in terms of proceeds, was the relief fund of the Association of Professional Ball Players of America.

Special guests

Some players documented the day's happenings by bringing movie cameras to the park. "What's the game coming to?" groused Frisch.

Celebrity sightings at the ol' ballpark included Hollywood's

★ 1940 ALL-STAR GAME ★

With first baseman George McQuinn grounded by a sore leg, the Browns failed to get a player into St. Louis' first All-Star exhibition.

George Raft, Bob Hope and Joe E. Brown.

The hometown Browns, who were in Detroit before the All-Star break and headed for New York immediately after it, were brought back to St. Louis at the team's expense to attend the game. According to *The Sporting News*, the club spent about $500 on transportation for players and scouts and lost about $2,000 in potential revenue by canceling two exhibition games that had been arranged. Brownies manager Fred Haney was spotted in the upper deck – not quite the Bob Uecker seats, but not exactly adjacent to the dugout, either.

Hometown scorecard

It didn't take long for the locals to get in on the action when the Midsummer Classic began. With the crowd inching forward, Cincinnati righthander Paul Derringer (an 18-game winner as a rookie for the Cardinals' 1931 World Series winner) delivered the first pitch of the game – and the Senators' Cecil Travis whacked it to deep center field, where Moore ran it down.

Unfortunately for hometown fans, it was one of the few highlights for St. Louis' All-Star contingent.

After the Nationals struck for three runs before a batter was retired in their half of the first, A.L. starter Red Ruffing finally got someone out – Mize, who flied to Red Sox left fielder Ted Williams.

Mize was the N.L.'s runaway leader at the break with 21 homers and ranked third with 53 RBIs. But he went 0-for-2 in the game, grounding out in his other at-bat. He was replaced by Reds first baseman Frank McCormick in the sixth.

Moore played all nine innings and recorded a second putout in the seventh inning, this one on a long smash by Boston first baseman Jimmie Foxx.

At the plate, he didn't fare much better than Mize. Batting eighth, he fouled out to Foxx in his first at-bat, in the second inning. In his three other trips, he flied out, drew a base on balls and struck out. Before coaxing the walk, he seemed none too pleased when Cleveland righthander Bob Feller twice came in high and tight.

McQuinn, meanwhile, was a no-go because of a painful nerve condition in his leg. His absence from game action meant that the Browns were the only team in the majors that failed to get a player into the 1940 contest. Through the eight All-Star Games played to that point, only three Browns had taken the field: outfielder Sam West, the A.L.'s starting left fielder in 1937 and a ninth-inning defensive sub in 1933 and '34; catcher Rollie Hemsley, the Americans' starting catcher in 1935; and outfielder Myril Hoag, a pinch-hitter in 1939.

Mixed message for 'Muscles'

Joe Medwick's first appearance at Sportsman's Park after being traded by the Redbirds in June came as the starting left fielder for the N.L. All-Stars. He was greeted by a loud mix of cheers and boos. Medwick made his first regular-season visit as a Dodger on July 20 – and launched a monstrous home run off the scoreboard in his first at-bat.

Medwick was a six-time All-Star as a Cardinal, making his first appearance in 1934. He starred in the 1937 game, setting an All-Star record with four hits.

Threat vs. promise

Former Brownie Bobo Newsom's threat not to pitch for the A.L. if bypassed as the starter was an All-Star prequel to Garry Templeton's "If I ain't startin', I ain't departin'" line, which the Cardinals' shortstop spewed in 1979 after he was named a reserve for the N.L. team. Newsom was just joshin'; Tempy wasn't.

Marketing visionary

While the All-Star Game was an unqualified success in the opinion of most observers, longtime New York baseball writer Dan Daniel proved to be a contrary sort, citing "certain deficiencies in the affair at Sportsman's Park." In the "Over the Fence" column that Daniel wrote for *The Sporting News,* he said the game "was played on a cold stage. Advance publicity was almost nil. Whoop-la by both leagues was missing woefully before and on the day of battle. Sportsman's Park was unadorned with bunting. The band showed up an hour before the game. Al Schacht (the baseball comedian) was missing."

Plans apparently had called for players from both teams to accompany a band onto the field for flag-raising ceremonies, but the marching orders never reached managers Joe Cronin and Bill McKechnie: The players didn't budge from their benches. Yet commissioner Kenesaw Mountain Landis wasn't displeased: "These people came out to see a ballgame, not a parade."

Looking ahead to the 1941 All-Star Game in Detroit, Daniel offered this prescient view of future Midsummer Classics: "Get the two squads out at Briggs Stadium for a workout the day before the game. Let there be, the day before the game, picture-taking interviews, writers talking with players and the two managers. Deck out your park in the national colors. Get two bands to blare their heads off from 10 in the morning to closing. When there are changes, announce where the new men are going to hit in the batting order. More information, more excitement, more wow. That's what the game needs." What, no home run derby?

— *Joe Hoppel*

In his first St. Louis appearance in Dodger blue, former Cardinal Joe Medwick didn't entirely feel the love he once inspired at Grand and Dodier.

★ 1940 ALL-STAR GAME ★

NATIONALLY FAMOUS

FALSTAFF

PREMIUM QUALITY

NATIONAL LEAGUE ALL-STARS | 1 2 3 4 5 6 7 8 9 10 R H E

5—Vaughan, 2—Jurges, 7—Miller, ss
4—Herman, 3—Coscarari, 2b
4—Ott, 4—West, rf
10—Mize, 10—McCormick, 1b
4—Lombardi, 9—Phelps, 8—Danning, c
7—Medwick, 1—J. Moore, lf
5—Lavagetto, 19—May, 3b
8—T. Moore, 9—Leiber, cf
30—Derringer, 11—Hubbell, 31—Walters, 14—French, 17—Wyatt,
9—Mulcahy, 14—Higbe, p

1—J. Moore, N.Y. 4—Lombardi, Cin. 7—Miller, Bos. 9—Phelps, Brk. 14—Higbe, Phil.
2—Durocher, Brk. 4—Ott, N.Y. 7—Medwick, Brk. 10—McCormick, Cin. 17—Wyatt, Brk.
2—Jurges, N.Y. 4—West, Bos. 8—Danning, N.Y. 19—May, Phil. 30—Derringer, Cin.
3—Coscarart, Brk. 5—Lavagetto, Brk. 11—Hubbell, N.Y. 31—Walters, Cin.
4—Herman, Chi. 5—Vaughan, Pitt. 9—Leiber, Chi. 14—French, Chi.

Manager: 1—McKECHNIE, Cin. Coaches: 1—Prothro, Phil., 32—Stengel, Bos.
Trainer: Rohde, Cin. Umpires: 1—Reardon, 2—Stewart.
Batting Practice Pitchers: 21—Warneke, St. Louis; 37—Shoffner, Cin. Batting Practice Catcher: 2—Gowdy, Cin.

AMERICAN LEAGUE ALL STARS | 1 2 3 4 5 6 7 8 9 10 R H E

2—Rolfe, 25—Keltner, 3b
9—Williams, 5—Greenberg, 4—Johnson, lf
9—Keller, 25—Finney, rf
5—DiMaggio, 8—Cramer, cf
3—Foxx, 5—McQuinn, 1b
4—Appling, 5—Boudreau, ss
6—Gordon, 6—Mack, 2b
8—Dickey, 8—Hayes, 9—Hemsley, c
19—Feller, 12—Newsom, 20—Milnar, 15—Ruffing,
10—Bridges, 16—Pearson, p

2—Rolfe, N.Y. 5—DiMaggio, N.Y. 8—Cramer, Bos. 9—Williams, Bos. 16—Pearson, N.Y.
3—Foxx, Bos. 5—Greenberg, Det. 8—Dickey, N.Y. 10—Bridges, Det. 19—Feller, Clev.
4—Appling, Chi. 5—McQuinn, St. L. 8—Hayes, Phila. 12—Newsom, Det. 20—Milnar, Clev.
4—Johnson, Phil. 6—Gordon, N.Y. 9—Hemsley, Clev. 15—Ruffing, N.Y. 25—Keltner, Clev.
4—Boudreau, Clev. 6—Mack, Clev. 9—Keller, N.Y. 16—Leonard, Wash.

Manager: 4—CRONIN, Bos. Coaches: 30—Daly, Bos., 32—Del Baker, Det.
Trainer: Win Green, Bos. Umpires: 3—Basil, 4—Pipgraf.
Batting Practice Pitcher: 32—Keefe, Phila. Batting Practice Catcher: 22—Berg, Bos.

AND HERE'S YOUR ALL STAR LINE-UP of

PEVELY Super Test DAIRY PRODUCTS

IRRADIATED HOMOGENIZED MILK CREAM IN EVERY DROP!

BUTTERMILK TRADITIONAL SUMMER COOLER!

DELICIOUSLY DIFFERENT ICE CREAM!

ORANGE DRINK MADE WITH FRESH ORANGES!

CHOCOLATE DRINK A REAL THIRST QUENCHER!

Pevely

THE ONLY DAIRY PRODUCTS SOLD IN SPORTSMAN'S PARK

The names of 18 future Hall of Famers graced the 1940 All-Star scorecard, including seven in the American League's starting lineup. Managers Joe Cronin and Bill McKechnie also earned plaques in Cooperstown.

Yankee obsession

When the American League team arrived at Sportsman's Park for the 1940 All-Star Game, it possessed two familiar components: more than a little swagger and more than a few New York Yankees. And, at first glance, why not? The Americans had been punishing the National League in World Series and All-Star Game competition, and the Yankees had played a big role in the mayhem.

Joe McCarthy's New York club had become such a force that the A.L. had made a bold attempt to level — maybe even bulldoze — the playing field during the Winter Meetings before the 1940 season, legislating that its defending league champion (the Yankees, of course) could not make a conventional trade with any club until it no longer was the reigning pennant-winner. (After the Tigers surprisingly won the '40 A.L. flag, the no-trade rule for the league's champs was rescinded, in July 1941.)

Strangely, the Bronx Bombers didn't seem to be their usual potent selves in 1940 — to the point where there was talk in St. Louis that the Yankees were in the midst of a collapse. When the A.L. All-Star team was announced on the last day of June, the Yankees stood at 32-32 and were described as faltering in one news account.

Despite New York's first-half struggles, the eight A.L. managers entrusted with selecting their league's 25-man roster named seven members of the fourth-place Yanks to the squad. In addition to the five Yankees who were eventually penciled into the starting lineup, pitcher Monte Pearson and third baseman Red Rolfe were selected for the roster. (Pearson didn't get into the game; Rolfe was sidelined with an eye ailment and replaced by Washington's Cecil Travis.)

Detroit had the most reason to grouse about the roster selections. The Tigers, who were atop the A.L. standings entering the All-Star Game, placed only three players on the roster. The second-place Indians fared better with six, including fireballer Bob Feller, who had tossed an Opening Day no-hitter and who, in the estimation of the *St. Louis Globe-Democrat*'s Bob Burnes, was "becoming more of an immortal with each performance."

Immortal or not, Feller didn't get the starting nod. In fact, when A.L. manager Joe Cronin revealed his starting lineup, not a single Detroit or Cleveland player was in the mix.

As for the National League roster, the Dodgers led the way with six players, followed by the Giants with five, although Giants shortstop Billy Jurges ended up deferring because of injury. The league-leading and defending N.L. champion Reds had four representatives.

Counter to the criticism directed toward the A.L. selection decisions, Boston Bees manager Casey Stengel – one of N.L. skipper Bill McKechnie's lieutenants for the game – boasted after the Nationals' victory that his league's managers "picked 'em pretty well, didn't we? Almost everybody we picked was used."

Phillies pilot Doc Prothro joined Stengel in assisting McKechnie for the game; Cronin's staff featured Tom Daly (a Red Sox coach) and Tigers manager Del Baker.

Lumber company

Several All-Stars were on a tear going into the Midsummer Classic. The Red Sox's second-year left fielder, a gent named Ted Williams, was penciled in as a starter in his first Dream Game appearance. He entered the game hitting a lusty .345. Red Sox teammate Lou Finney was leading the A.L. in batting, at .359.

Tigers outfielder Hank Greenberg entered the break with 71 RBIs, and the Red Sox's Jimmie Foxx had 68. Moreover, Boston's first baseman distinguished himself by becoming the only player selected to all eight All-Star Games. The 1940 classic was his fourth as a starter.

A slip-up occurred late in the game when Greenberg and the Red Sox's Finney (who, like Greenberg, was an A.L. sub) batted out of order. However, nothing of consequence occurred to induce McKechnie to issue a protest.

Paid no heed

The Yankees' Lefty Gomez, the Red Sox's Lefty Grove and the Tigers' Charlie Gehringer were among the former All-Star headliners passed over for the 1940 game. Gehringer's .500 average (10-for-20) in six All-Star appearances led all active players who had appeared in at least three Dream Games. Gomez had started five of the first six Midsummer Classics, en route to a pair of records that still held up entering 2009: most All-Star victories (three) and most starts (five, equaled by two others).

Some of the 1940 season's better hitters also were spurned during the selection process. Of the top five men in the batting race in each league at the break, only one – the White Sox's Luke Appling – was an All-Star starter. Five others – the Dodgers' Dixie Walker, the Cubs' Jimmy Gleeson, the Browns' Rip Radcliff, the White Sox's Taft Wright and the Tigers' Barney McCosky – weren't selected for the game, even as reserves.

Max-imum effort

Max West's injury raised the specter of an All-Star Game hex, conjuring memories of Cardinals ace Dizzy Dean's toe fracture in the 1937 classic and Reds outfielder Ival Goodman's shoulder injury in the 1939 game. But West was back in his Boston team's lineup when regular-season play resumed, two days after he rammed into Sportsman's Park's right-field wall.

One lineup card in which West's name would never again appear: the one presented at the All-Star Game. His career All-Star record: one game, one at-bat, one game-turning home run.

Once more, with vengeance

The A.L.'s dominance of the N.L. coming into the game sparked plenty of chatter before, during and after the 1940 All-Star showdown.

Much was made in the press about how the Nationals' victory in St. Louis was their second of the year over the Americans. The first was a 2-1 St. Patrick's Day triumph in Tampa, in a game that was

★ 1940 ALL-STAR GAME ★

patterned after the All-Star Game and involved players from teams whose spring training camps were in Florida.

So low was the N.L.'s esteem in the spring – its World Series representative had been swept the previous two Octobers – that *The New York Times'* headline for the game screamed, "National League Upsets American." Sure, it was March, and indeed, it was an exhibition game, but the outcome nonetheless was deemed a major surprise – one the N.L. could savor. The Cards' Terry Moore helped make the

victory possible, laying down a ninth-inning bunt that set up the game-winning hit by Brooklyn's Pete Coscarart.

When the bona fide All-Star event rolled around in July, the two teams seemed to take very different approaches to the game. *St. Louis Star-Times* sports editor Sid Keener noted that the American Leaguers "walked to their positions for the first time with a lackadaisical strut" and were "oh so nonchalant about everything." Not letting up, he suggested "several of those $20,000-a-year boys seemed bored over the

---

Former All-Star fixtures Lefty Gomez and Dizzy Dean, pictured before they squared off as starters at the 1937 gala, were among members of the old guard absent in 1940. Gomez had started five of the first six summer classics.

entire proceedings." In Keener's mind, the Nationals were keyed up, "determined to give the best they had, despite the fact no blue-ribbon championship hinged on the result."

During the entire A.L. batting practice session, McKechnie delivered a pep talk to his National League troops. N.L. president Ford Frick was busy, too, handing out an assortment of gifts to his charges. First-year members of the Nationals received an $85 wristwatch, second-year participants accepted silver plaques and perennial selections got cigarette cases.

If there was any doubt about how much the N.L. wanted to win the midsummer event, it was erased by what news reports labeled a "mob scene" in the clubhouse after the Nationals nailed down their 4-0 victory. One reporter said president Frick "wore a smile so broad that it threatened his ear lobes." *The New York Times* again used the word "upset" in a headline to describe the outcome at Grand and Dodier.

The Americans weren't exactly in distress over the loss. Several players pointed out the league's superiority in the World Series – where the "big cash is on the line."

Still no say for fans

The A.L. managers' botched job of picking their roster appeared to signal an imminent return to voting by the fans, who had chosen the All-Star teams in 1933 and '34 (with some fine-tuning allowed by the managers). The switch was even reported to be a done deal, with most observers certain that fans' interest in the game would soar if they were back in the business of selecting the players. Yet the major league owners eventually reversed course, and fans didn't choose the teams again until 1947.

Famed journalist Red Smith, then with the *Philadelphia Record*, called the owners "meddlesome" for taking the vote away from the fans in the first place, writing "they couldn't be bothered with the columns of publicity to be gained through a nationwide vote of fans." Smith also offered these broadsides: "The customer's place was a $1.14 seat behind a stanchion" – a vantage point from which he was to "keep his big yap shut." Had Sportsman's Park fans had a say in the matter, Smith went on, it's unlikely there would have been so many Yankees on hand – "but they weren't asked."

Post-break wrapup

In September, Foxx hit a hallowed milestone, becoming the second player in major league history – behind Babe Ruth – to reach the 500-homer plateau.

The Tigers and Reds went the distance in the postseason, with Cincinnati clinching its second World Series championship with a Game 7 victory in front of its home crowd. Derringer picked up the victory, while fellow All-Star hurler Bobo Newsom was dealt the loss.

Oh, and as for those fast-fading, washed-up Yankees? They caught fire and finished two games behind the A.L. champion Tigers, then returned to their World Series championship throne in 1941.

– Joe Hoppel

The only participant picked for the first eight All-Star Games — a streak that reached nine — Jimmie Foxx became the majors' second 500-homer slugger.

★ 1940 ALL-STAR GAME ★

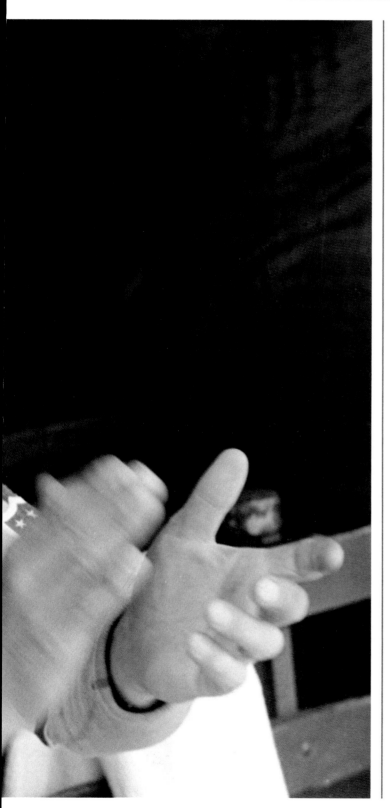

"Meet Me in St. Lou-iee, Lou-iee, Meet Me at The Game!" – so shouted the headline atop the front page of *The Sporting News*, the self-proclaimed Baseball Paper of the World, in the issue previewing the 1940 All-Star Game. St. Louis was badly in need of some kind of exclamation point to the '40 baseball season, a dreary one at that point for backers of the Cardinals and Browns.

That the Brownies were in sixth place at the All-Star break was hardly a surprise; they'd totaled 411 losses over the previous four seasons and hadn't had a winning campaign since 1929. But the Redbirds' presence on the same rung of the second division was a shocker. The club had shown flashes of potential – including a seven-homer explosion May 7 – but back-to-back doubleheader losses at home to Frankie Frisch's Pirates on the Saturday and Sunday before the All-Star Game dropped the Cardinals to 27-40.

No question, the Redbirds had made plenty of news in the five weeks preceding the All-Star Game, but not much of it was positive.

• Coming off a second-place finish in 1939 under new manager Ray Blades, the Cards were 10 games below .500 on June 7 when owner Sam Breadon announced he was replacing Blades with Billy Southworth.

"We hated to do this," Breadon said, "because Blades is as fine a fellow as you'll find. But the way things have been going, we simply had to make a change."

Blades had taken over after the club finished sixth in 1938, a year in which Frisch, the old Gas House Gang leader, was let go late in the season in his final go-round at the Cardinals' helm.

Southworth, summoned from St. Louis' Rochester farm club, had played for the Cardinals' 1926 World Series champions and managed the Cards for part of the 1929 season.

• On June 12, two days before Southworth formally assumed the managerial reins from interim boss Mike Gonzalez, the Cardinals

★ 1940 ALL-STAR GAME ★

A half-season turnaround in 1940 under new Cardinals manager Billy Southworth paid even bigger dividends with pennants in '42, '43 and '44.

Terry Moore, OF
Cardinals

1940
NATIONAL
LEAGUE
STARS

Frank McCormick, 1B
Reds

Bucky Walters, P
Reds

Billy Herman, 2B
Cubs

CARDINALS AT SPORTSMAN'S PARK

July 11 (N), 13† (2) . . . . .New York		Aug. 22, 23, 24† . . . . .Philadelphia
July 14* (2), 15, 16 (T. B. Day) . . . . . . .Boston		Aug. 25* (2), 26 (N), 27 . . . . .Boston
July 17 (N), 19 (2) . . . . .Philadelphia		Aug. 28, 29 . . . . .New York
July 20†, 21* (2) . . . . .Brooklyn		Sept. 4 (N), 6 . . . . .Chicago
Aug. 14 (N), 16 (2) . . . . .Pittsburgh		Sept. 7†, 8* (2) . . . . .Pittsburgh
Aug. 17†, 18* (2) . . . . .Cincinnati		Sept. 24, 25, 26 . . . . .Cincinnati
Aug. 20 (2), 21 . . . . .Brooklyn		Sept. 27, 28†, 29* . . . . .Chicago

†Indicates Saturday Games   *Indicates Sunday Games   (N) Indicates Night Games

CARDINAL NIGHT GAMES

Thursday, July 11 . . . . .New York
Wednesday, July 17 . . . . . .Philadelphia
Wednesday, August 14 . . . . .Pittsburgh
Monday, August 26 . . . . .Boston
Wednesday, September 4 . . . . . .Chicago

CARDINAL DOUBLE HEADERS

Saturday, July 13 . . . . .New York
Sunday, July 14 . . . . .Boston
Friday, July 19 . . . . .Philadelphia
Sunday, July 21 . . . . .Brooklyn
Friday, Aug. 16 . . . . .Pittsburgh
Sunday, August 18 . . . . .Cincinnati
Tuesday, August 20 . . . . .Brooklyn
Sunday, August 25 . . . . .Boston
Sunday, September 8 . . . . .Pittsburgh

TICKETS ON SALE DOWNTOWN TICKET OFFICE
Mezzanine Floor — Arcade Building
Telephones: CH. 7984   Long Distance 99
ADDRESS MAIL ORDERS: CARDINAL TICKET OFFICE, P. O. DRAWER 15, ST. LOUIS, MO.

jolted their fans by trading outfielder Joe Medwick to the Dodgers in a six-player deal that also sent $125,000 St. Louis' way.

Medwick, who had won the Triple Crown in his MVP season of 1937, had become an unhappy camper in St. Louis, believing that he wasn't being paid a salary commensurate with his skills. Outfielder Ernie Koy was the key player the Redbirds obtained in the swap.

• Three days before Blades' dismissal, 23,500 fans had turned out for the first home night game in club history. What was meant to be a festive occasion turned ugly when fans littered the field with bottles after a series of umpires' calls – and the Cardinals' shoddy play – sent them over the edge. Brooklyn won, 10-1. The one bright spot under the Sportsman's Park lights: Medwick's 5-for-5 spree.

The Browns had beaten the Cardinals to the punch as night-baseball hosts, playing their first Sportsman's Park game under the lights on May 24. During the All-Star goings-on, the *St. Louis Post-Dispatch* stressed that night ball was proving a big boost to the Browns' attendance – so much so that speculation about a possible relocation of the franchise was lessening.

Down the stretch

When play resumed after the All-Star Game, the Cardinals came alive under Southworth. Johnny Mize, one of the team's two All-Star Game representatives, hit for the cycle in the first game of a July 13 doubleheader against the Giants, sparking a stretch in which St. Louis won nine of 10 games.

The Redbirds reached .500 in early August, treaded water for two weeks, and then finished with a 31-16 flourish.

All told, St. Louis was 57-29 after the break, 69-40 under Southworth and 84-69 at season's end – good for third place in the National League. Mize fueled the second-half sprint, driving in 84 runs after the break. He concluded the season as the N.L. leader in RBIs (137) and home runs (a franchise-record 43).

The Browns, who were 33-44 when the Midsummer Classic came to town, finished 67-87 and in sixth place. Despite their 11th consecutive year in the second division, the Brownies showed marked improvement after a 43-111, last-place disaster in 1939, when they set an American League record by finishing 64½ games out of first place.

Outfielder Rip Radcliff, unfazed by his All-Star snub, continued to pound the ball in the second half of the season; he finished the year with 200 hits (tied for the league lead) and a .342 average (fourth in the A.L.).

– *Joe Hoppel*

A page from the 1940 All-Star Game program (opposite) promoted two big attractions on the Cardinals schedule: night baseball and doubleheaders. Johnny Mize (above) finished the season as the N.L. leader in RBIs and home runs.

★ 1940 ALL-STAR GAME ★

★1948 ALL-STAR GAME ★

AMERICAN LEAGUE 5, NATIONAL LEAGUE 2

SPORTSMAN'S PARK, JULY 13

"I'm really sorry the American League won't be at full strength tomorrow, because we'll get no credit for winning," a National Leaguer complained on the eve of the 1948 All-Star Game in St. Louis. "Everyone will say we beat their junior varsity."

True, the Americans' starting lineup on July 13 would be missing three gifted players who had been voted in by the fans – injured stars Ted Williams (Boston), Joe DiMaggio (New York) and George Kell (Detroit). Their designated starting pitcher, Hal Newhouser (Detroit), also would be forced to the sidelines by injury, after initially being chosen by A.L. manager Bucky Harris to start the Midsummer Classic for a second straight year.

Yet when the 15th All-Star Game ended amid thunder, pelting rain and brisk winds at Sportsman's Park, no one was cracking wise about how the National League had managed a rare All-Star victory only

because it was fortunate enough to face the scrubs edition of the A.L. squad. And for the best of reasons: The N.L. couldn't get it done, even against an American team that not only was racked with injuries, but also was battered by turmoil from within. The Nationals went down ingloriously, 5-2.

Sportsman's Park was packed to the roof to witness another victory by the American League, which extended its All-Star record to 11-4.

1948 ALL-STAR GAME

With would-be starters (from left) Hal Newhouser, George Kell, Ted Williams and Joe DiMaggio limited by injuries, the Americans were considered ripe for a rare upset by the National League.

As demoralizing and almost embarrassing as the day was for the National League – its record dropped to 4-11 in these glitter fests – it featured at least one uplifting moment for St. Louis fans, provided they didn't dawdle while getting to their seats. It came minutes after the game's 1:35 p.m. first pitch, when Stan Musial slammed the first of a record six All-Star Game homers he'd hit in his career, and the first in All-Star history hit by a National Leaguer playing in his home park.

Harris had been expected to start either Vic Raschi or Joe Page – both from his own Yankees staff – in place of Newhouser. Instead, the skipper opted for the Washington Senators' Walt Masterson, who quickly ran into a heap of trouble. The Phillies' Richie Ashburn swung at the game's first pitch – the N.L. was the visiting team, because the Browns were playing Dream Game host for the first, and only, time – and the rookie center fielder beat out an infield roller. After Ashburn stole second, Cardinals second baseman Red Schoendienst advanced him to third with a groundout to the right side.

Up stepped Musial, who at age 27 already had won two N.L. batting titles and two league Most Valuable Player awards and was in the midst of not-so-arguably one of the greatest seasons in big-league history. The matchup of Masterson vs. Musial – the righthander had a 6-6 record entering the game, while Musial was batting .403, with 20 home runs and 65 runs batted in – proved no match at all when the Cardinals superstar and crowd favorite launched a monstrous drive onto the pavilion roof in right-center field, setting off a roar in the stands.

"I wasn't particularly set on hitting a homer," Musial said. "I just wanted to drive in that runner ahead of me, so I took my natural swing."

That swing just might have bordered on supernatural, considering Stan's revelation that batting in Sportsman's Park (which the Cardinals shared with the Browns) was not business as usual on this day. "It was awfully hard to see up there at the plate because of the white shirts in the center-field stands," he explained. "Our club doesn't seat fans out there, but I guess it's OK to sell those seats for the All-Star Game...."

The Nationals seemed primed to add to their 2-0 lead when the New York Giants' Johnny Mize followed Musial's smash with a single and Enos Slaughter, the Cards' third starter in the game, drew a walk. But Masterson escaped further havoc, getting Andy Pafko (Cubs) and Walker Cooper (Giants) to hit into successive forceouts.

Still, the American League was down early, and it appeared to lack the resources – and just maybe the cohesiveness – to battle back with its trademark gusto.

Williams (rib injury) and DiMaggio (leg problems) would be available at best for pinch-hitting duty; Kell (sprained ankle) was a no-go.

Bob Feller's decision to pull out of the game for the second year in a row (in 1947, he cited a back injury, although he pitched 8⅓ innings two days after that All-Star Game) not only deprived the Americans of another valuable weapon, but also touched off some nastiness between Harris and the Cleveland triumvirate of Feller (who said he simply wasn't available this time around), player/manager Lou Boudreau (who was the Americans' starting shortstop) and club owner Bill Veeck. With his decision to withdraw, the Indians ace appeared to raise to a boil the heated issue of player defections from the All-Star Game.

Then there was the unexpected loss of Newhouser because of arm soreness. The news came the day after Harris had named Newhouser the starter; while making that announcement, the manager couldn't resist taking a swipe at Feller.

"Naturally, our main objective is to win the game," Harris had said before heading to St. Louis. "And with that in mind I am starting Newhouser, who, you can be sure, will be there. Unlike Mr. Feller, Newhouser not only is a pitcher you can count on to be present for an All-Star Game, but will give you all he's got."

Newhouser, the majors' co-leader in victories with 13, was at Sportsman's Park for the game, but he wasn't able to throw (he didn't pitch again until the following weekend).

All told, the A.L. camp seemed in disarray, or at least distracted, for the 1948 classic. With matters not exactly going his way early in the game, Harris needed Masterson to steady himself and for the A.L.'s key reinforcements – Tommy Henrich (Yankees) in left field for Williams, Hoot Evers (Tigers) in center for DiMaggio and Ken Keltner (Indians) at third base for Kell – to provide some semblance of the offense usually supplied by the men they replaced.

Bingo. Masterson had a 1-2-3 second inning and wriggled out of

A.L. manager Bucky Harris (above, right) shook things up by looking outside his Yankees rotation and tabbing Walt Masterson (below, left) as his starting pitcher. N.L. skipper Leo Durocher (above, left) opted for a known commodity, countering with Ralph Branca (below, right) from his Dodgers staff.

a two-on, two-outs situation in the third. Henrich, Evers and Keltner were in the mix on offense – Henrich in a bizarre way, to be sure – when the Americans struck for five runs over a three-inning span.

Evers, who wasn't a big bopper in the DiMaggio or Williams mold but had pounded three home runs for Detroit in a five-day span shortly before the break, lined a one-out shot into the left-field bleachers in the second inning. The homer, which came off N.L. starter Ralph Branca of the Brooklyn Dodgers, didn't elicit the response that Musial's blow did. Yet the moment had a distinctly local flavor, considering that Evers, a star high school athlete a decade earlier in nearby Collinsville, Ill., had been on the radar of area fans even before Stan the Man arrived in St. Louis.

The A.L. then tied the score off Branca in the third. Pinch-hitter Mickey Vernon (Senators) and right fielder Pat Mullin (Tigers) drew walks to start the inning. Branca caught Henrich looking on strike three – normally a good thing for the team in the field, right? Ah, but history tells us that good things can happen to the offensive team when Henrich strikes out – remember

Staking the Nationals to a 2-0 lead, Stan Musial cracked the first All-Star home run by a National Leaguer playing in his home ballpark.

catcher Mickey Owen's World Series-turning muff in 1941 as Henrich fanned? Vernon and Mullin worked a double-steal on the strikeout pitch, which put runners in scoring position and left N.L. third baseman Pafko holding the bag but not covering it.

As *New York Times* columnist Arthur Daley pointed out, the double-steal would never have occurred if the Cubs' Pafko, a converted outfielder, "hadn't been asleep at the switch. Perhaps no one ever bothers to steal against the Bruins, since there are easier ways of scoring on them. At any rate, Pafko stood engrossed in his thoughts a few feet off the bag while Vernon slid around him."

Boudreau followed Pafko's gaffe with a fly ball that drove in Vernon, and the game was deadlocked.

The rival managers' ensuing pitching choices proved to be game-changing. Harris' No. 2 man was Raschi, a righthander who had compiled a 10-3 record in the first half of the season; N.L. manager Leo Durocher selected Cubs lefthander Johnny Schmitz, who was only 8-9 at the break but had beaten Leo's Dodgers three times.

The decision to bring in Schmitz raised some eyebrows – the N.L. had such stalwarts as Johnny Sain (Braves) and Ewell Blackwell (Reds) available – and absolutely floored *Sporting News* correspondent Stan Baumgartner.

"Charlie Grimm or someone with the Cubs should have told Leo Durocher that Schmitz can't pitch with two days' rest," wrote Baumgartner, alluding to Schmitz's complete-game outing against

congratulated on the novelty of a pitcher providing the winning hit in an All-Star Game. Though he'd been going well on the mound all season, Raschi admitted to being in a funk of late at the plate – until his at-bat against Schmitz.

The Nationals, who appeared almost dumbstruck over what had unfolded at Sportsman's Park, felt they couldn't catch a break – a pitcher beating them with his bat, Pafko committing a mental blunder, a rookie outfielder making the egregious mistake of leaving the bat on his shoulder in a key situation and golden opportunities being wasted – but *The Sporting News* probably captured their fate best with its "N.L. Guilty of Dumb Ball" headline.

Mize searched for words to sum up yet another long day for the N.L., then offered this: "How are you going to figure on a thing like a pitcher getting the big hit of the ballgame?" Wistfully, he added: "Boy, I sure thought we had 'em after that first inning."

No such luck. Not even against the American League's jayvee squad.

Joe Hoppel is a free-lance writer based in St. Louis.

A pair of local legends celebrated their first All-Star selections, Yankees catcher Yogi Berra (above, right) and Detroit outfielder Hoot Evers, who homered in his first at-bat. One-man wrecking crew Vic Raschi (below) drove in the Americans' go-ahead runs and pitched three shutout innings.

---

the Pirates on the Saturday before Tuesday's All-Star extravaganza. "Warren Brown, veteran Chicago scribe, said that everyone in the Windy City knows that unless Schmitz has four days' rest, he can't throw hard enough to get Aunt Kate out."

After the N.L. went meekly in the top of the fourth against Raschi, it was Aunt Katie-bar-the-door in the bottom half.

Keltner got things shaking with a one-out single down the third-base line, and former Brownie George McQuinn, now in Yankee pinstripes, singled to right-center. Then, as the mostly pro-N.L. crowd cringed, Schmitz walked Birdie Tebbetts (Red Sox), who was hitting eighth and had just taken over defensively at catcher for Buddy Rosar (Philadelphia Athletics). Raschi was scheduled to bat next, but with DiMaggio and Williams possibly able to swing the bat, would Harris use a pinch-hitter at this key juncture, despite Raschi's mere one inning of work?

Harris said he never considered hitting for Raschi, explaining after the game "that boy's likely to poke one at any time." And poke one he did, into left field, allowing Keltner and McQuinn to scamper home. Durocher had seen enough, and he waved in Sain; Harris countered with DiMaggio, who batted for Mullin and delivered a lineout to Musial in left that scored Tebbetts.

The game was scoreless the rest of the way, with the National League blowing a big chance in the sixth when it loaded the bases. But Raschi was as good with his arm as he was with the bat, getting the 21-year-old Ashburn on a called third strike to end the inning. The Athletics' Joe Coleman then held the N.L. hitless over the final three innings.

"Hasn't it been done before?" a surprised Raschi responded when

★ 1948 ALL-STAR GAME ★

JULY 13, 1948

Sportsman's Park

A.L. 5, N.L. 2

National League	AB	R	H	RBI	BB	SO	American League	AB	R	H	RBI	BB	SO
Richie Ashburn (Phillies) CF	4	1	2	0	0	1	Pat Mullin (Tigers) RF	1	0	0	0	1	1
Ralph Kiner (Pirates) LF	1	0	0	0	0	0	c-Joe DiMaggio (Yankees) PH	1	0	0	1	0	0
Red Schoendienst (Cardinals) 2B	4	0	0	0	0	0	Al Zarilla (Browns) RF	2	0	0	0	0	0
Bill Rigney (Giants) 2B	0	0	0	0	1	0	Tommy Henrich (Yankees) LF	3	0	0	0	1	2
Stan Musial (Cardinals) LF, CF	4	1	2	2	1	1	Lou Boudreau (Indians) SS	2	0	0	1	0	0
Johnny Mize (Giants) 1B	4	0	1	0	0	1	Vern Stephens (Red Sox) SS	2	0	1	0	0	1
Enos Slaughter (Cardinals) RF	2	0	1	0	1	0	Joe Gordon (Indians) 2B	2	0	0	0	0	0
Tommy Holmes (Braves) RF	1	0	0	0	0	0	Bobby Doerr (Red Sox) 2B	2	0	0	0	0	1
Andy Pafko (Cubs) 3B	2	0	0	0	0	0	Hoot Evers (Tigers) CF	4	1	1	1	0	1
Bob Elliott (Braves) 3B	2	0	1	0	0	0	Ken Keltner (Indians) 3B	3	1	1	0	1	0
Walker Cooper (Giants) C	2	0	0	0	0	0	George McQuinn (Yankees) 1B	4	1	2	0	0	0
Phil Masi (Braves) C	2	0	1	0	0	0	Buddy Rosar (Athletics) C	1	0	0	0	0	0
Pee Wee Reese (Dodgers) SS	2	0	0	0	0	1	Birdie Tebbetts (Red Sox) C	1	1	0	0	2	1
Buddy Kerr (Giants) SS	2	0	0	0	0	1	Walt Masterson (Senators) P	0	0	0	0	0	0
Ralph Branca (Dodgers) P	1	0	0	0	0	0	a-Mickey Vernon (Senators) PH	0	1	0	0	1	0
b-Frank Gustine (Pirates) PH	1	0	0	0	0	1	Vic Raschi (Yankees) P	1	0	1	2	0	0
Johnny Schmitz (Cubs) P	0	0	0	0	0	0	e-Ted Williams (Red Sox) PH	0	0	0	0	1	0
Johnny Sain (Braves) P	0	0	0	0	0	0	f-Hal Newhouser (Tigers) PR	0	0	0	0	0	0
d-Eddie Waitkus (Cubs) PH	0	0	0	0	1	0	Joe Coleman (Athletics) P	0	0	0	0	0	0
Ewell Blackwell (Reds) P	0	0	0	0	0	0	**Totals**	**29**	**5**	**6**	**5**	**7**	**7**
g-Bobby Thomson (Giants) PH	1	0	0	0	0	1							
Totals	**35**	**2**	**8**	**2**	**4**	**7**							

National League	2	0	0		0	0	0		0	0	0	–	2	8	0
American League	0	1	1		3	0	0		0	0	x	–	5	6	0

National League	IP	H	R	ER	BB	SO	HR	BF	American League	IP	H	R	ER	BB	SO	HR	BF
Ralph Branca (Dodgers)	3	1	2	2	3	3	1	13	Walt Masterson (Senators)	3	5	2	2	1	1	1	15
Johnny Schmitz (Cubs) L	0.1	3	3	3	1	0	0	5	Vic Raschi (Yankees) W	3	3	0	0	1	3	0	13
Johnny Sain (Braves)	1.2	0	0	0	0	3	0	5	Joe Coleman (Athletics)	3	0	0	0	2	3	0	11
Ewell Blackwell (Reds)	3	2	0	0	3	1	0	14	**Totals**	**9**	**8**	**2**	**2**	**4**	**7**	**1**	**39**
Totals	**8**	**6**	**5**	**5**	**7**	**7**	**1**	**37**									

a-Walked for Masterson in third. b-Struck out for Branca in fourth. c-Flied out for Mullin in fourth, scoring Tebbetts from third.
d-Walked for Sain in sixth. e-Walked for Raschi in sixth. f-Ran for Williams in sixth. g-Struck out for Blackwell in ninth.
LOB: NL 10, AL 8. HR: Musial, Evers. SB: Ashburn, Vernon, Mullin, McQuinn. SH: Coleman. WP: Masterson. Umpires: Changed
positions in fifth to: HP - Beans Reardon, 1B - Joe Paparella, 2B - Bill Stewart, 3B - Charlie Berry. Time: 2:27. Attendance: 34,009.

Scottrade®

RELIABLE. STABLE. TRUSTED.

J.D. Power and Associates has Ranked Scottrade the
"Highest in Investor Satisfaction with Self-Directed Services."*

(800) 619-SAVE |  | **www.scottrade.com**

Here For You Since 1980. Online Since 1996.

Resident All-Stars

The Cardinals may have been visitors to Sportsman's Park on this occasion – the Browns were official All-Star Game hosts, and the A.L. franchise owned the ballpark – but there were birds perched on bats everywhere you looked.

The nationwide vote of fans landed two Cardinals in the N.L.'s starting lineup: left fielder Stan Musial, who trailed only Boston's Ted Williams in overall balloting, and right fielder Enos Slaughter, who edged the Braves' Tommy Holmes in a close vote.

N.L. manager Leo Durocher added three more Redbirds to his roster: second baseman Red Schoendienst, shortstop Marty Marion and pitcher Harry Brecheen. The injury bug came into play for all three of those additions.

Schoendienst, though bothered by nagging injuries and limited to pinch-hitting duty of late, slid into a starting role when the Braves' Eddie Stanky suffered a fractured ankle five days before the game.

As owners of Sportsman's Park, the Browns festooned their ballpark in classic Americana on a stifling day that had Cleveland executives Bill Veeck (above, left) and Hank Greenberg feeling additional heat over Indians ace Bob Feller's absence from St. Louis.

From the scene at the ballpark to the buzz around town, St. Louis' host–city role helped define the 1948 All–Star experience.

★ 1948 ALL-STAR GAME ★

The only member of the host club on the Americans' roster, Browns outfielder Al Zarilla ranked third in the A.L. batting race at All-Star time.

Cards had three others in uniform for the game. Manager Eddie Dyer served as the Nationals' third-base coach, and relief ace Ted Wilks and backup catcher Del Wilber worked as N.L. batting-practice batterymates.

St. Louis' other team wasn't represented nearly as well. The Browns were shut out from the A.L.'s starting lineup, and manager Bucky Harris chose right fielder Al Zarilla as the only Brownie on the roster. Zarilla was hitting a cool .332 at the break, the third-best figure in the A.L.

Yankees coach Johnny Schulte, a St. Louis native and former Brownie and Cardinal, caught B.P. for the Americans. The Yankees' regular catcher, St. Louis Hill native Yogi Berra, was on hand after being named to his first-ever All-Star squad. Inactive during the game, Berra had hosted a party at the Chase Hotel the previous night to formally announce his engagement to childhood sweetheart Carmen Short.

Drawing a crowd

Hotel space was tight for the All-Star Game; the arrival of 1,200 delegates for the Poultry and Egg Board national convention made it even tighter. Both teams and baseball's upper-echelon executives were headquartered at the Chase Hotel.

Ticket prices for the game were listed as: $5, $4, $2.50 (standing room), $1.50 and $1. Scalpers were offering not-so-choice tickets – $1 bleacher seats – for $20. After the game got under way, though, the going rate dropped to 50 cents.

Neat as a pin

The Browns held a contest to design the commemorative press pins distributed to the newspaper and radio personnel assigned to cover the game. St. Louisan Lawrence Lisitano pocketed $100 for his winning proposal, which emulated the look of the Browns' cap.

Ten other designs received honorable mention laurels, good enough to land each entrant a reserved-seat ticket for the classic. More than 100 entries were submitted, and the winners were chosen by editorial cartoonists from the city's three daily newspapers and the locally-based sports weekly *The Sporting News*.

Making the scene

Taken to task by some for the no-frills appearance of the ballpark for the 1940 All-Star Game, St. Louis got no such criticism this time. Sportsman's Park was colorfully adorned with the flag-like banners that everyone had come to expect for baseball's showcase events.

The pregame atmosphere proved lively, as well. Fans obviously were eager to see baseball's crème de la crème – and up close, if possible. The *Star-Times* reported a strange pregame scene in which "the playing field somehow was overrun with women, children, autograph seekers, police and most everyone except the persons who should be there – those carrying accredited press credentials." Commissioner Happy Chandler surveyed the confusion and ordered the field cleared.

Musial and A.L. counterpart Ted Williams posed for photographers before the game. "No, Ted didn't ask me for any

Marion withdrew from the game because of a cranky back, a decision that came under some fire. Marion had seemed fine two days before the All-Star Game – when he collected St. Louis' lone hit against Cincinnati's Ken Raffensberger – and he was in the Cards' lineup in their first game after the break. Unquestionably, Bob Feller's absence from the classic at Sportsman's Park made pulling out a touchy subject.

Brecheen, who had started the season with three consecutive shutouts (and missed a perfect game in his third start because of a scratch hit), was not used by Durocher. A report in the *St. Louis Star-Times* indicated the lefthander was held out because of a strained wrist.

In addition to having five All-Stars chosen for the roster, the

Leading their leagues in hitting at the break, the Cardinals' Stan Musial and the Red Sox's Ted Williams were bound for batting titles at season's end.

tips on batting," said Musial, tongue presumably planted firmly in cheek. The Red Sox star, while not in the .400 stratosphere like Stan was at the break, was hitting a gaudy .388, coming off a Triple Crown the previous season.

Dizzy Dean – who had "unretired" to start the last game of the 1947 season for the Browns in a publicity stunt – also was on hand at Sportsman's Park, regaling listeners with tales of barnstorming matchups against Satchel Paige, whom the Cleveland Indians had just signed.

Eye on the sky

One St. Louis sportswriter noted the popularity of sunglasses in the crowd, saying it reflected on the "novelty of day baseball in St. Louis." The Cardinals and Browns, with 45 and 40 night games scheduled, respectively, for the '48 season, ranked 1-2 in the majors in that category. Six of the other 14 big-league clubs had as few as 14 nighttime games on their schedules.

As the day wore on, those sunglasses would be replaced by rain gear. The weather started out sunny and, in the words of Dean, "hotter than a depot stove." But ominous clouds and thunder arrived early in the proceedings, and the wind whipped up in the sixth inning. However, the weather mostly cooperated until the downpour at game's end.

Because of the threat of rain in the forecast, the cover had been left on the field until the last moment at the suggestion of N.L. president Ford Frick. When the cover was taken off the field an hour before the game, though, the ground appeared too dry, and the infield had to be watered down. Players took batting practice but skipped infield drills.

Television debut

KSD-TV in St. Louis became the first outlet anywhere to televise an All-Star Game, using two cameras behind first base to beam the game to area fans. In May, the commissioner's office – sensing the potential of the new medium of television – had approached NBC-TV about showing the game nationally, but the network said it lacked a "cable connection" with St. Louis and didn't think a film presentation of the game would be profitable. Also, NBC had committed to televising the Democratic National Convention, whose gathering in Philadelphia coincided with the All-Star Game. NBC suggested the game be televised locally, and KSD-TV (now KSDK) – which had been on the air for only 17 months – was at the ready.

Sudden impact

St. Louis continued to prove hospitable to All-Star Game newcomers, particularly ones with local ties. In 1940, Boston Bees outfielder Max West had become the first player ever to homer in his first All-Star at-bat; in this game, St. Louisan and Collinsville High product Hoot Evers became the second. The Detroit player went deep in the second inning.)

Collinsville native Art Fletcher, a longtime Yankees coach, gave the Illinois community another prominent face at the game. Fletcher stopped by the A.L. dugout to wish Harris good luck.

Hometown scorecard

In addition to his first-inning homer, Musial delivered a broken-bat single in the third inning. However, his ensuing baserunning miscue helped the Americans escape the inning unscathed. When the next batter, the Giants' Johnny Mize, grounded to second baseman Joe Gordon (Indians), Musial stopped short in his slide, allowing Lou Boudreau, who initially muffed Gordon's relay flip, to retrieve the ball for a forceout. Slaughter followed with an infield single, which would have loaded the bases with one out. As it was, Andy Pafko then bounced into an inning-ending forceout.

Musial ended up 2-for-4 at the plate, with one walk.

As for other St. Louis players in the game, Slaughter went 1-for-2, including a walk. His hell-bent manner of hustle came to the fore in the fourth, when he narrowly averted a collision with an usher in a vain attempt to run down a ball deep in foul territory.

Schoendienst wore the collar in four at-bats, making him 0-for-6 in two career All-Star starts. Zarilla entered the game in the fifth inning and played the rest of the way, going 0-for-2 in what would be his lone All-Star appearance.

– Joe Hoppel

Red Schoendienst made his second start in as many All-Star appearances.

CHANGE YOUR OIL, PROTECT YOUR INVESTMENT.

Get **Castrol EDGE** our most advanced synthetic oil, providing your car with both performance and protection. Or for proven power technology try **Castrol SYNTEC**. Use **Castrol GTX** for superior protection against sludge build-up.* And for superior oil burn-off protection **Castrol GTX High Mileage**.**

* 5W-30 and 10W-30 grades.
** Versus leading conventional oils.

Available at:

IT'S MORE THAN JUST OIL. IT'S LIQUID ENGINEERING.™

The Feller flap

The explanation came a little late to get his ace pitcher off the hook, but it did come eventually: "The only thing I'm interested in is winning a pennant for Cleveland."

With those words, Indians owner Bill Veeck drove home the point that the All-Star Game would not get in the way of achieving his goal. That meant the 1948 American League All-Star team could use one of the two Indians pitchers selected by A.L. manager Bucky Harris for the game, but not both. And therein lay a big-time controversy, which started three days before the game when the league office announced it had been notified that Cleveland fireballer Bob Feller "would not be available" to pitch in St. Louis.

Feller caught a lot of heat for the withdrawal. Harris, for one, couldn't contain his displeasure with the Indians hurler – whom he claimed would never get another All-Star invitation as long as he had anything to do with the selection process – saying that players on other teams "are just as sore as I am. They are just mad enough to point for Bob and the Indians the rest of the season. Sometimes just ordinary men play over their heads when aroused."

The criticism was understandable. Feller, who could be a recalcitrant sort, had excused himself from the 1947 game because of a questionable injury, and now he was pulling out again – for reasons that had nothing to do with his health.

Veeck, who initially had little to say about the Feller brouhaha, tried to clear the air at an owners meeting held in conjunction with the All-Star Game. "I told him (Feller) not to pitch in the game," disclosed Veeck, who added: "I saw no reason for selecting two of our pitchers. They picked both Feller and (Bob) Lemon, and Lemon is here."

That didn't appear to be great consolation to Harris. The A.L. skipper said Lemon really didn't figure into his All-Star pitching plans, never mind the fact the Cleveland righthander had tossed a no-hitter against Detroit on June 30 and shared the major league lead with 13 victories.

Although Feller continued to get pummeled

Heeding the call of his employer, Cleveland's Bob Feller backed out of his second consecutive All-Star Game.

for his absence – some observers wondered if Veeck was taking a bullet for a superstar employee who thought the All-Star Game was a waste of time – the pennant-race factor was hard to ignore. The first-place Indians were nursing a half-game lead over the Philadelphia Athletics and a 2½-game edge on Harris' Yankees going into the break, and Feller and Lemon had pitched complete games in a doubleheader against the Browns two days before the All-Star clash. (Feller lost, dropping his record to 9-10, while Lemon tossed a shutout, improving to 13-7.)

Of course, Feller wasn't alone on the "I can't make it" list; the Cardinals' Marty Marion also caused a stir when he withdrew from the game late, claiming back problems. Commissioner Happy Chandler was none too pleased, and weighed in on player defections – past, present or future – during his visit to St. Louis: "I am very much concerned over the failure of club owners and players to take seriously the All-Star Game.... We have had some straight talk. I assume that in the future every player who is voted on the All-Star team will show up. We have no plan to punish anybody, but we will take whatever steps are necessary."

Two A.L. superstars who were clearly ailing but made the trip, Ted Williams and Joe DiMaggio, took part in the game as pinch-hitters. Williams drew a walk, and DiMaggio drove in a run when he lined out to Musial in left field.

Another man who refused to be kept down was umpire Beans Reardon, who persevered with his assignment despite a bad cold.

"I couldn't let folks say that umpires are ducking this game, too," he said.

Fulfilling the fans' will

The nation's fans, who in 1947 had been brought back into the All-Star selection process, cast more than 4 million votes in '48 in a three-week poll conducted by the *Chicago Tribune* and 452 other

A pregame show of force by National League sluggers (from left) Johnny Mize, Walker Cooper, Ralph Kiner and Stan the Man ultimately proved punchless after Musial's first-inning homer.

★ 1948 ALL-STAR GAME ★

newspapers, publications and radio stations nationwide. Fans chose the starting lineups, excluding pitchers; managers picked their own mound staffs and, basing their decisions largely (but not entirely) on the results of fan balloting, also selected the reserve players for the 25-man rosters. Williams, Stan Musial and DiMaggio ranked 1-2-3 in the fans' voting. Williams garnered 1,556,784 votes, Musial 1,532,502 and DiMaggio 1,519,182.

Fans chose two starters each from five teams – the Yankees (center fielder DiMaggio and first baseman George McQuinn), Indians (shortstop/manager Lou Boudreau and second baseman Joe Gordon), Tigers (third baseman George Kell and right fielder Pat Mullin), New York Giants (first baseman Johnny Mize and catcher Walker Cooper) and Cardinals (left fielder Musial and right fielder Enos Slaughter).

The Cards and Indians wound up with three starters each when Redbirds second baseman Red Schoendienst filled in for injured Eddie Stanky of the Braves and Cleveland third baseman Ken

Keltner replaced the hobbled Kell. The latter move put Indians at three of the four positions on the A.L.'s starting infield.

N.L. manager Leo Durocher shook things up by picking only six pitchers, opting to load up on offensive players – including three third basemen behind starter Andy Pafko of the Cubs – in hopes of outslugging the Americans. Yet Leo bypassed the Reds' Hank Sauer, whose 24 homers led the majors at the break. "Great is the wailing, and vigorous the gnashing of teeth, in Cincinnati," *The Sporting News* reported. Sauer had finished third in voting for N.L. left fielders.

Durocher's coaches were Cardinals manager Eddie Dyer and Giants boss Mel Ott. Harris' braintrust was Bronx-centric – he tapped Yankees coaches Chuck Dressen and John (Red) Corriden.

Closing a cultural chapter

In one highly significant way, the 1948 All-Star Game in St. Louis was exactly like the 14 Midsummer Classics that had

N.L. manager Leo Durocher (center) joined forces for a day with the dugout bosses of the Dodgers' chief rivals, Eddie Dyer (right) of the Cardinals and Mel Ott of the New York Giants.

Commissioner Happy Chandler (behind bunting) accorded first-pitch honors to Burt Shotton, a former Cardinals and Browns outfielder who managed Brooklyn to the 1947 National League pennant.

preceded it. And, heading into the 2009 extravaganza at Busch Stadium, it was unlike any of the 64 that have followed. America was changing, and so was baseball's showcase event.

The '48 All-Star contest – for all the immense talent that was on hand at Sportsman's Park – still didn't include black players, whose emerging major league presence would help alter the nation's societal landscape and at the same time take the skill level of baseball's greatest players to an even higher plane. The Dodgers' Jackie Robinson, who had integrated the modern major leagues in 1947 and captured Rookie of the Year honors in the process, was having another fine year in 1948 –

he was hitting .295 at the break – but didn't make the National League squad. But Robinson, Brooklyn teammates Roy Campanella and Don Newcombe (who reached the majors in '48 and '49, respectively) and Cleveland's Larry Doby (who, like Robinson, made his debut in '47) became the All-Star Game's first black participants in the landmark 1949 contest at Ebbets Field.

So, as the 2009 All-Star Game approaches, the 1948 game in St. Louis has become a historical footnote – the last All-Star clash in which no black players performed.

All-Star keepsake

The honor of throwing out the first ball went to Burt Shotton, who had managed the Dodgers to the pennant in 1947 after Durocher had been suspended for the season by Chandler for "conduct detrimental to baseball." With Leo back on the job in Brooklyn, Shotton served as an honorary manager for this All-Star Game. At the insistence of Chandler, Shotton kept the first-pitch ball as a memento.

Shotton – a former outfielder with both the Browns (1909, '11-17) and Cardinals (1919-23) – wasn't the only one to walk away from Sportsman's Park with a special souvenir. The players spent 20 minutes before the game autographing baseballs, with each All-Star receiving two balls as a keepsake.

Unlucky elephants

The N.L. appeared to be in a great position to score a rare victory in the Midsummer Classic, thanks to the A.L.'s lengthy injury list. Cracked *Collier's* magazine writer Bill Fay: "The Republicans and National League are in the same fix. If they don't win this year, they never will." As it turned out, both GOP presidential candidate Thomas E. Dewey and the N.L. All-Stars managed to snatch defeat from the jaws of victory.

A money pitcher

Braves righthander Johnny Sain, boasting an 11-6 record en route to a final mark of 24-15, was asked to meet with Boston club officials on the morning of the game. Told he was getting a pay hike, the ecstatic Sain went out and retired all five A.L. hitters he faced. He struck out the side in the fifth inning.

Not a one-hit wonder

Winning A.L. pitcher Vic Raschi, who got the game's big hit, was on his way to a 19-hit, 11-RBI season for the Yankees – not bad for a hurler. Also impressive: a seven-RBI game he had later in his career while pitching for the Yanks.

Six years later in St. Louis, Raschi would become a trivia note. Pitching for the Cardinals at home against Milwaukee on April 23, 1954, he yielded the first of Hank Aaron's 755 home runs.

No sacrifice

Though Boudreau and DiMaggio collected RBIs when retired on their third- and fourth-inning drives to the outfield, they nonetheless were charged with at-bats. The sacrifice-fly rule, formerly a part of the game, was still off the books and wouldn't be adopted again until 1954.

More Feller fallout

Harris pulled the Indians' middle-infield combination of Boudreau and Gordon in the fifth – reports indicated he considered doing so in the fourth inning – as his feud with Cleveland showed little sign of letting up.

The A.L. skipper also got the Tigers' Hal Newhouser into the game as a pinch-runner, a move that was viewed in some quarters as a symbolic slap at Feller. The thinking went that Harris was emphasizing that Newhouser, though hurting physically, had willingly made the trip to St. Louis and then contributed in any way he could; not so for that hale-and-hearty Feller fella.

Playing the blame game

Once Harris' men had defeated Durocher's, there was carping from on high. "Now, I'm not complaining about the loss, but I believe the system of picking the team is wrong," N.L. president Ford Frick said. "If they want to continue this vote of the fans, that's all right, but they should not handcuff the manager by insisting that he has to play the starting lineup chosen by the fans for three innings. Take the case of Andy Pafko. He's a nice guy and I like him. But he hasn't the experience to play third base in a game of this kind. He showed it when he failed to take the throw properly from Walker Cooper in the third inning (when a double-steal helped the A.L. tie the game).... I believe the manager should have the full say about the makeup of the team on the field at all times. Bob Elliott (Braves) would have been our third baseman then and the results might have been different."

Pafko, who was hitting .342 at the break, had been exclusively an outfielder in his minor and major league career until being switched to third base by the Cubs in the spring.

Post-break wrapup

Three days after the All-Star Game, a bombshell announcement was made in New York – Durocher was leaving the Dodgers to replace Ott as Giants manager, and Shotton was returning to the Brooklyn helm.

On Aug. 16, baseball mourned the loss of its most revered figure, Babe Ruth, who died at age 53. Among the many accomplishments in his storied career, Ruth hit the first home run in the history of the All-Star Game, connecting against the Cardinals' Bill Hallahan in the inaugural classic in 1933.

Also in August, Satchel Paige, the longtime Negro leagues and barnstorming pitcher who had joined the Indians just before the All-Star break, threw back-to-back shutouts. *The Sporting News* was among the outlets that had blasted the signing of Paige, who supposedly was 39 years old, probably was 42 and might have been 50. "To sign a hurler at Paige's age is to demean the standards of baseball in the big circuits," said the St. Louis-based weekly, which considered the transaction a mere publicity stunt and insisted Paige would not have drawn interest if he were white.

Satch finished the season with a 6-1 record and 2.48 ERA. He would be selected to the 1952 and 1953 A.L All-Star teams while with the Browns and would pitch one inning in the '53 classic.

Even if A.L. teams played with more intensity against the Indians after the All-Star Game ruckus – as Harris suggested they might – Cleveland could not be stopped. The Indians won the pennant in a one-game playoff with the Red Sox, then beat the Braves in the World Series. En route, they set a regular-season attendance record in the majors, drawing 2,620,627 fans.

– Joe Hoppel

★ 1948 ALL-STAR GAME ★

Deca SPORTS™

10 COMPLETE SPORTING EVENTS
AVAILABLE NOW!

$29.99

2-4 PERSON MULTIPLAYER ACTION

Wii™

HUDSON
www.decasports.com

St. Louis fans had plenty to boast about – and something to fret about – when their city played host to the 1948 All-Star Game. Stan Musial was having a career year – which is saying something, considering the numbers he put up over 22 major league seasons – and was clearly *the* star among All-Stars when baseball's best players and top dignitaries descended upon Sportsman's Park for the July 13 game.

Musial entered the break with a .403 average, leading the National League's No. 2 hitter, Philadelphia rookie Richie Ashburn, by more than 50 percentage points. The Cards outfielder had collected an N.L.-high 120 hits in 76 games (which included one tie), knocked in a league-best 65 runs and blasted 20 homers (No. 3 in the N.L.). The Triple Crown – last won in the N.L. by another Cardinal, Joe Medwick, in 1937 – seemed within range.

The good tidings extended to the team as a whole. The Redbirds – coming off a second-place finish in 1947 and two years removed from a World Series championship – were in third place with a 39-36 mark. Despite 10 losses in their last 14 games, the club appeared capable of contending throughout the season.

All seemed positive for the Cardinals franchise, which eight months earlier had been purchased from longtime owner Sam Breadon by a syndicate headed by U.S. postmaster general Robert E. Hannegan, a native St. Louisan, and Fred M. Saigh Jr., a St. Louis attorney. The price tag of approximately $4 million marked the highest figure ever paid for a big-league franchise.

Things were not so cheery with the Browns, whose wartime success (a pennant in 1944 and third-place finishes in '42 and '45) obviously was an aberration. They were buried in seventh place in the American League standings with a record of 28-45, and their flagging gate posed a threat to St. Louis' status as a two-team major league city.

Idle in the All-Star Game, Harry Brecheen won 20 games in 1948 and topped the league in ERA, strikeouts and shutouts.

Overshadowed by Musial's epic season, Enos Slaughter knocked in 90 runs and ranked in the league's Top 5 in batting and hits.

It didn't help that in the previous offseason the Browns had unloaded such core players as Vern Stephens, Jack Kramer, Bob Muncrief, Walt Judnich, John Berardino and Ellis Kinder in cash-laden deals that bolstered the club's coffers but hurt the team on the field and alienated what few fans it had.

A turnout of 2,787 for a June 23 game against the Philadelphia A's set off Browns owner Richard Muckerman, who said he would consider transferring the franchise unless the team received greater fan support. Acknowledging he already had received offers to move the club, Muckerman said, "I've always turned them down, hoping that, sooner or later, our St. Louis fans would rally around our Browns. But now I'm beginning to wonder if they will."

Down the stretch

The Cardinals' 46 victories after the break were second-most in the league — and second-best is where they finished in the standings, 6½ games behind the Braves.

Musial hit .351 in the second half, hammering 19 homers and amassing 66 RBIs in the process. If his post-All-Star break batting average disappointed those hoping for an epic ".400" season, Stan's overall numbers did not. He finished with a .376 average, 230 hits, 135 runs, 46 doubles, 18 triples, 131 RBIs, a .450 on-base average (not yet an official statistic) and a .702 slugging average — all league-leading figures. His home run total of 39 left him one behind the Pirates' Ralph Kiner and the Giants' Johnny Mize — and deprived Musial of the Triple Crown.

Another dazzling statistic: Musial had more homers than strikeouts (34). The monstrous production resulted in his third MVP award, the last of his career.

Musial wasn't alone in having a big year. Pitcher Harry Brecheen won 20 games and led the N.L. in ERA (2.24), shutouts (seven) and strikeouts (149); Enos Slaughter batted .321 (fifth in the N.L.), rapped 176 hits (fourth) and knocked in 90 runs. Both placed among the top 10 in MVP voting (Brecheen was fifth, Slaughter tied for seventh).

★ 1948 ALL-STAR GAME ★

Browns executives William (right) and Charles DeWitt moved into the owners' office after the 1948 season, taking over a club that had averaged fewer than 4,400 fans per game.

The end of the season marked the end of the line for two longtime Cards favorites. In a nine-day span beginning in late September, the team released Joe Medwick, who had re-joined the club in 1947, and Terry Moore, a Redbird since 1935.

The Browns wound up sixth in the A.L. at 59-94. Right fielder Al Zarilla finished with a .329 batting average and third baseman Bob Dillinger hit .321, the fourth- and sixth-best marks in the league.

The Brownies' attendance figures, though, proved to be the most telling numbers for the club. The American Leaguers attracted only 335,546 fans – the Cardinals had drawn a million-plus for the third consecutive season – and in February 1949 a beaten-down Muckerman sold the Browns to William O. DeWitt Sr., the club's vice president-general manager (and father of the current Cardinals chairman and CEO) and his brother Charles, the team's traveling secretary.

By 1954, three years before St. Louis would serve as All-Star host for the third time, the city would be home to only one major league club, the Browns having relocated to Baltimore.

– *Joe Hoppel*

PITCH IN: HOME AND AWAY

Eco-Shape® Bottle

LESS PLASTIC · BETTER ENVIRONMENT

Join the team and help make a difference by recycling

THE OFFICIAL BOTTLED WATER OF THE CARDINALS

Cardinals

A little natural does a lot of good.®

*Based on an August 2008 national audit of half-liter plastic bottles across the tea, soda and water categories, the Eco-Shape® half-liter bottle contains an average of 30% less plastic versus comparable size, leading beverage brands.

©2009 Nestlé Waters North America Inc.   PSPONS14225_05

 PLEASE RECYCLE

★ 1957 ALL-STAR GAME ★

AMERICAN LEAGUE 6, NATIONAL LEAGUE 5

SPORTSMAN'S PARK, JULY 9

Wishfully scripted as a Musial vs. Williams epic, the 1957 All-Star Game survives voters' casting misdeeds to deliver a rousing ninth-inning climax.

First, Ford Frick took center stage. Then it was Minnie Minoso's turn.

Who knew?

The spotlight at the 1957 All-Star Game in St. Louis supposedly would shine most brightly on Stanley Frank Musial and Theodore Samuel Williams. After all, the July 9 gala at Grand and Dodier was being billed as perhaps the final head-to-head meeting between two of baseball's greatest players in a meaningful game – or at least the last go-round in which the extraordinarily gifted veterans would still be playing with consummate skill.

Did we say meaningful game? The All-Star Game? Well, yes. Most folks took the game very seriously a half-century ago. Except, that is, for those cutup fans in Cincinnati, who for the second straight year made a mockery of the voting process and stuffed the ballot box. This time, they crammed it to overflowing and beyond.

Enter commissioner Frick. After watching with dismay as a late avalanche of votes from southern Ohio thrust Redlegs players into the lead at all eight position-

player spots for the National League team, Frick said whoa. He ruled that no matter how the final tally wound up, the Cardinals' Musial (first base), the Giants' Willie Mays (center field) and the Braves' Hank Aaron (right field) would start over Cincinnati's George Crowe, Gus Bell and Wally Post.

(Musial did overtake Crowe in the voting, but Mays and Aaron couldn't catch Bell and Post.)

Even though Cincinnati still landed five players in the N.L. starting lineup (as it did in 1956, when unbridled voter enthusiasm and a radio station's campaign did the trick without a landslide), Frick's decisive action had rescued the game from potential farce status. It also shifted pregame attention back where it belonged – to Musial and Williams, who would be appearing in their 14th and 13th All-Star Games, respectively, and doing so on Stan's home grounds.

Musial, 36, ranked third in the N.L. batting race at the break with a

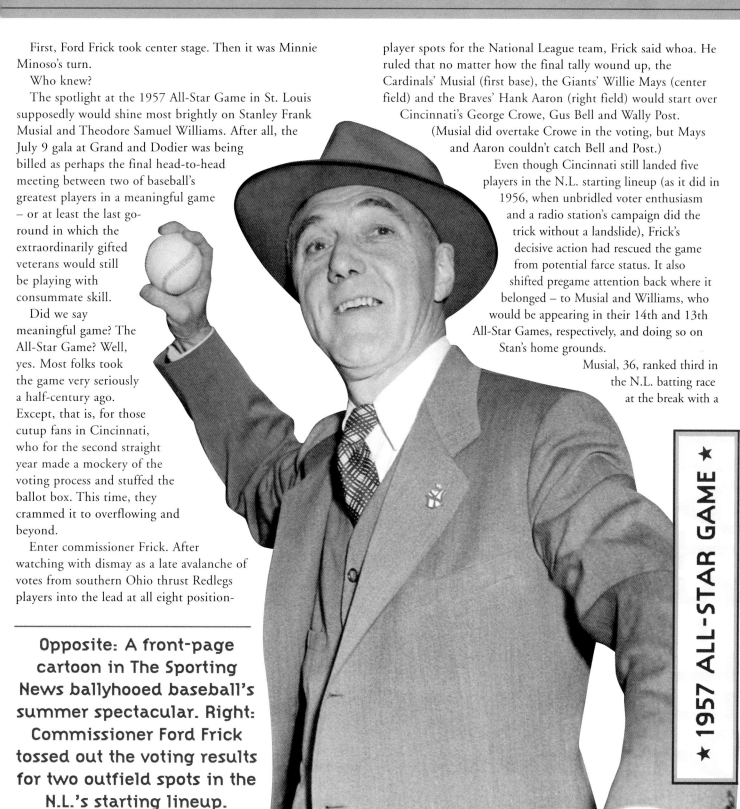

Opposite: A front-page cartoon in The Sporting News ballyhooed baseball's summer spectacular. Right: Commissioner Ford Frick tossed out the voting results for two outfield spots in the N.L.'s starting lineup.

★ 1957 ALL-STAR GAME ★

dealing – and dominating. The Yankees skipper's original choice to start and stifle had been Early Wynn (11-10 record), but the 37-year-old Indians workhorse had logged seven innings just two days before the All-Star clash and thus was available only for abbreviated relief duty.

Stengel had an exemplary Plan B starter in mind: Detroit's Jim Bunning, who already had beaten every other team in the league on the way to a 10-2 record and 2.03 ERA. Still, Stengel thought Wynn's savvy would have served the A.L. well from the starting spot, and his displeasure with Cleveland for using Wynn so close to the big game – rookie manager Kerby Farrell was directing the Indians in '57 – was reminiscent of the Yankees-Indians rift the last time the All-Star Game was held in St. Louis. That time, A.L. manager Bucky Harris, also of the Yankees, was livid about all things Cleveland when Indians ace

.341 average; in All-Star competition, he was batting .319 with five home runs. Williams, 38, was second in the '57 A.L. batting derby with a .343 mark; he entered the classic with a .361 career All-Star mark and four home runs. Both players had homered in the previous year's game, while Musial had connected two years earlier for a game-ending blast in the 12th inning.

As Old Lady Fate would have it, though, neither of baseball's grand old men left much of a mark on the 24th All-Star Game. Oddly enough, Williams' late-game replacement, the White Sox's Minoso, was the player who left his fingerprints all over this one.

But before Minnie did his thing, there was a whole lot of not much going on at Busch Stadium (as old Sportsman's Park was now called) – unless, of course, you prefer standout pitching and stellar defense to good hitting and any sense of drama. In fact, until the ninth inning, the most riveting moment connected with this edition of the classic had come when Frick made his game-saving play nearly two weeks before the teams took the field.

A.L. manager Casey Stengel, determined to get the Americans back on track after six losses in the previous seven All-Star Games, was only too happy to keep the game reasonably devoid of pulsating moments if it meant his pitchers were wheeling and

The skippers and their first mates — Casey Stengel (left) and Walter Alston (right) flank starting pitchers Jim Bunning and Curt Simmons.

Bob Feller withdrew from the 1948 game.

"It isn't that I have anything against starting Bunning," Stengel said. "He has been going great ... but I still would like to have used Wynn. I would like to see a rule passed forbidding any manager from starting a pitcher chosen for the All-Star Game two days before the game."

Though Ol' Case wasn't forced to deal with a landslide-driven starting lineup like the one confronting N.L. manager Walter Alston of the Dodgers, the A.L. skipper was irked that he had to open the game with the fans' choices of Vic Wertz (Indians) at first base, Harvey Kuenn (Tigers) at shortstop and George Kell (Orioles) at third base, all of whom had slipped a bit after solid starts to the season. "Right now, I would say the Red Sox's third baseman, Frank Malzone, is about the hottest player in our league," Stengel said. "Yet I can't start him."

The A.L. manager complaineth too much. Wertz, in fact, drove in the Americans' first run with a second-inning single off N.L. starter Curt Simmons (Phillies), and Kuenn collected an RBI later in the frame when his bases-loaded walk against Lew Burdette (Braves) forced in Williams, who was aboard via a base on balls. And Bunning was merely spectacular.

Pitching his first full season in the majors – he had appeared in a total of 30 games and made 11 starts in the previous two years – the 25-year-old righthander lacked experience but little else. He proved his mettle against the Nationals, retiring all nine batters he faced and not once shaking off catcher Yogi Berra of the Yankees. He was in such a groove that he later admitted, "I know that the rule prohibits a pitcher from working more than three innings ... but I would have liked to continue today."

No need – not with Baltimore's Billy Loes waiting in the wings. The former Dodger had some anxious moments, but he still managed to face only two batters over the limit in his three-inning stint. In the N.L. fourth, Aaron reached base on a one-out single and Musial followed with a double to right, but Loes retired Mays on a pop-up and got Cincinnati's Ed Bailey on a groundout. In the fifth, an inning in which he eventually induced a double-play grounder, Loes luckily avoided a two-on, no-out situation when Cincy's Frank Robinson, who had led off the inning with a single, held up on Eddie Mathews' sinking liner to right field and was forced out at second after Detroit's Al Kaline trapped the Milwaukee player's smash. In the sixth, Loes watched as Kaline, his back against the wall, leaped to snare a drive by Red Schoendienst, the longtime Cardinals favorite who was now with the Braves.

By the time Loes departed, the Americans had extended their lead to 3-0. They scored in the top of the sixth when the Yankees' Bill Skowron banged a double off the right-field wall against Phillies rookie sensation Jack Sanford and Berra singled him home. It was Yogi's first RBI in 29 All-Star at-bats.

Now possessing what seemed like a safe cushion against an N.L. team

Banished from the starting lineup by Frick, Gus Bell belted a two-run pinch-double that woke up a dormant N.L. offense.

that had managed only three hits, Stengel summoned Wynn in the seventh, believing that the man he had wanted all along – fresh or not – was up to the task of delivering capable short relief.

Short it was; capable it wasn't. After Musial lined to the Yanks' Mickey Mantle to begin the inning, Mays and Bailey rapped singles and Bell, lopped off the starting lineup by Frick but added as a reserve by Alston, rammed a two-run pinch-double down the left-field line.

The Americans' comfort level was gone – and so was Wynn, who gave way to White Sox lefthander Billy Pierce. Mathews advanced Bell to third with a grounder, but the Cubs' Ernie Banks struck out against his crosstown rival.

Wynn had no alibis, denying he was gassed from the lack of rest. The problem, he said, was that "my fastball was not fast and my curve didn't curve. I didn't have a thing out there."

Cardinals righthander Larry Jackson had no such problems, keeping the Nationals in the game with scoreless relief in the seventh and eighth innings. His appearance was the first by a Cardinals pitcher in an All-Star Game played in St. Louis – and, heading into the 2009 Dream Game in the Gateway City, remains a singular event in the franchise's All-Star history. Jackson was helped by Mays' sensational running catch of a Williams smash to left-center in the eighth – a play that dazzled most at Busch but didn't strike Boston's Splinter as particularly splendid. Allowing it was a "nice catch," Ted nonetheless harrumphed: "I think every center fielder in our league would have caught the ball." Yes, league pride was a bit more evident – and the A.L.-N.L. rivalry a little more intense – in the '50s.

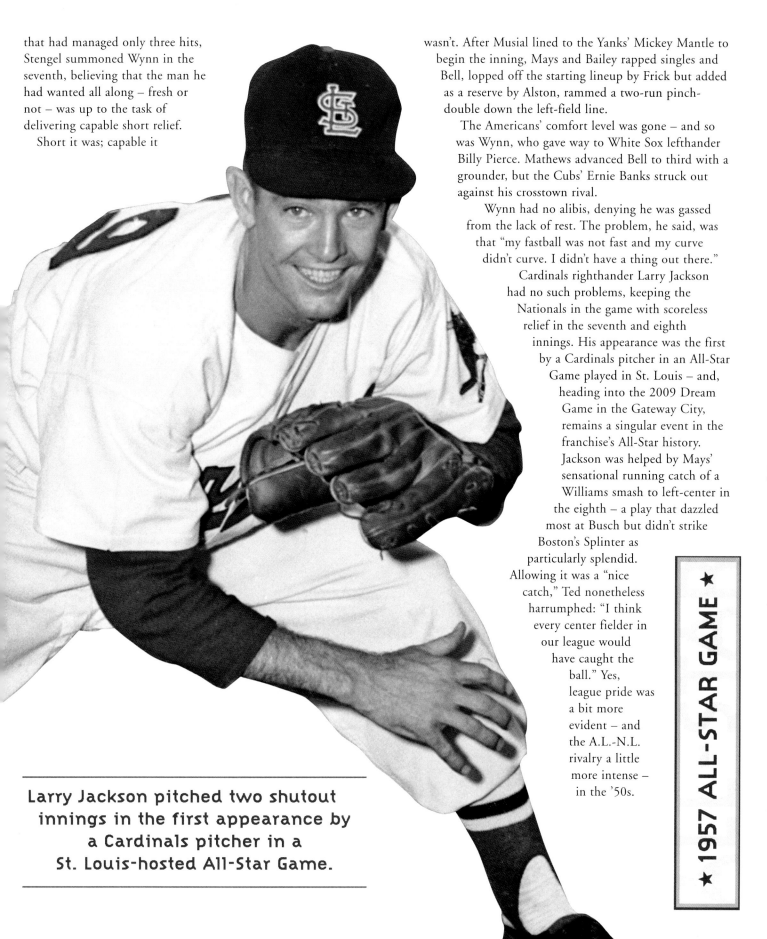

Larry Jackson pitched two shutout innings in the first appearance by a Cardinals pitcher in a St. Louis-hosted All-Star Game.

★ 1957 ALL-STAR GAME ★

Heads-up defense, a run scored and two RBIs distinguished Al Kaline's nine All-Star innings.

Williams' removal from the game for defensive purposes in the Nationals' eighth disappointed most fans – even though he wasn't likely to bat again, his departure put an end to the day's captivating Williams-vs.-Musial story line. But the insertion of Minoso in his place would prove telling in the ninth, a remarkably suspense-filled inning that overshadowed most of what had transpired earlier in the afternoon.

Alston decided to bring in Clem Labine, his own Brooklyn relief ace, in the ninth, and familiarity bred trouble. Pierce reached base on an infield hit, and Gil McDougald (Yankees) followed with a bouncer past the mound that second baseman Schoendienst fumbled in his haste to turn a double play. After Nellie Fox (White Sox) moved the runners over with a sacrifice, Kaline drilled a two-run single to left-center that gave the Americans a 5-2 lead.

Mantle struck out, but Minoso – getting a chance to swing the bat when Williams' No. 5 slot in the order came around again in the extended inning – tacked on what would be the game's decisive run with a double to right-center that scored Kaline.

Though Williams had finished his day's work, Musial was still gainfully employed, and The Man walked to lead off the Nationals' ninth. Mays rifled a triple into the right-field corner, scoring Musial, and Willie darted home when Pierce uncorked a wild pitch with pinch-hitter Hank Foiles (Pirates) at the plate.

It was now 6-4, A.L., and a single by Foiles and a walk to Bell put the potential tying runs aboard with no one out. Cleveland's Don Mossi took over for Pierce, and he fanned Mathews. (Second-guessers wondered whether Eddie should have been bunting.) Banks then singled past third baseman Malzone, the ball skipping into left field and setting off a chain reaction of events: Foiles scored on the play, Bell tried to leg it from first to third but was nailed on a bull's-eye throw by the alert Minoso, and Banks motored into second.

"Minnie made a whale of a throw to Malzone to get Bell," Alston said. "It had to be a perfect throw, and that's what he made."

The A.L. edge now down to 6-5, Stengel and Alston put the game in the hands of their trusted charges – the Yankees' Bob Grim came on to pitch and the Dodgers' Gil Hodges was sent up as a pinch-hitter. With a deadlocked game only a base hit away, Hodges smoked a liner to left field, which Minoso hauled in with a fine running catch. Game over.

Williams summed up the late-game goings-on best, telling Stengel, "You got me out of there just in time." No one doubted him. Ted's arm would have been no match for Minoso's on the play on Bell at third base, and his lack of speed might well have put Hodges' liner in play. And then there was Minoso's double that gave the American League its final run.

With the crowd focused intently on Williams and Musial all afternoon – Ted wound up 0-for-3 with a base on balls and a run scored, Stan went 1-for-3 with a walk and a run – Minoso had figured he'd spend the game in the same role as any of the 30,693 fans: that of mere spectator. "When the seventh inning come, I think I going to have vacation today," he said. "It sure feels good for the American League to win again."

Indeed, Minoso's impact on the outcome of the game in a scant inning and a half was a feel-good story in itself. The only thing rivaling it was Frick's impact on the integrity of the game before it was ever played.

Joe Hoppel is a free-lance writer based in St. Louis.

Right: A ninth-inning variety show of bat, arm and glove earned Minnie Minoso a game-ball memento. **Below:** Stengel's pregame anxiety ended with his second All-Star victory and postgame kudos from Cardinals manager Fred Hutchinson.

★ 1957 ALL-STAR GAME ★

JULY 9, 1957

Sportsman's Park

A.L. 6, N.L. 5

American League	AB	R	H	RBI	BB	SO
Harvey Kuenn (Tigers) SS	2	0	0	1	1	0
Gil McDougald (Yankees) SS	2	1	0	0	0	0
Nellie Fox (White Sox) 2B	4	0	0	0	0	0
Al Kaline (Tigers) RF	5	1	2	2	0	0
Mickey Mantle (Yankees) CF	4	1	1	0	1	1
Ted Williams (Red Sox) LF	3	1	0	0	1	0
Minnie Minoso (White Sox) LF	1	0	1	1	0	0
Vic Wertz (Indians) 1B	2	0	1	1	0	0
Bill Skowron (Yankees) 1B	3	1	2	0	0	0
Yogi Berra (Yankees) C	3	0	1	1	1	0
George Kell (Orioles) 3B	2	0	0	0	0	0
Frank Malzone (Red Sox) 3B	2	0	0	0	0	0
Jim Bunning (Tigers) P	1	0	0	0	0	0
a-Charlie Maxwell (Tigers) PH	1	0	1	0	0	0
Billy Loes (Orioles) P	1	0	0	0	0	0
Early Wynn (Indians) P	0	0	0	0	0	0
Billy Pierce (White Sox) P	1	1	1	0	0	0
Don Mossi (Indians) P	0	0	0	0	0	0
Bob Grim (Yankees) P	0	0	0	0	0	0
Totals	37	6	10	6	4	1

National League	AB	R	H	RBI	BB	SO
Johnny Temple (Reds) 2B	2	0	0	0	0	1
e-Red Schoendienst (Braves) PH-2B	2	0	0	0	0	0
Hank Aaron (Braves) RF	4	0	1	0	0	1
Stan Musial (Cardinals) 1B	3	1	1	0	1	0
Willie Mays (Giants) CF	4	2	2	1	0	1
Ed Bailey (Reds) C	3	1	1	0	0	0
h-Hank Foiles (Pirates) PH	1	1	1	1	0	0
Frank Robinson (Reds) LF	2	0	1	1	0	0
f-Gus Bell (Reds) PH-LF	1	0	1	2	1	0
Don Hoak (Reds) 3B	1	0	0	0	0	0
b-Eddie Mathews (Braves) 3B	3	0	0	0	0	1
Roy McMillan (Reds) SS	1	0	0	0	0	0
c-Ernie Banks (Cubs) PH-SS	3	0	1	1	0	1
Curt Simmons (Phillies) P	0	0	0	0	0	0
Lew Burdette (Braves) P	1	0	0	0	0	0
Jack Sanford (Phillies) P	0	0	0	0	0	0
d-Wally Moon (Cardinals) PH	1	0	0	0	0	0
Larry Jackson (Cardinals) P	0	0	0	0	0	0
g-Gino Cimoli (Dodgers) PH	1	0	0	0	0	1
Clem Labine (Dodgers) P	0	0	0	0	0	0
i-Gil Hodges (Dodgers) PH	1	0	0	0	0	0
Totals	34	5	9	4	2	6

	1	2	3	4	5	6	7	8	9		R	H	E
American League	0	2	0	0	0	1	0	0	3	–	6	10	0
National League	0	0	0	0	0	0	2	0	3	–	5	9	1

American League	IP	H	R	ER	BB	SO	HR	BF
Jim Bunning (Tigers) W	3	0	0	0	0	1	0	9
Billy Loes (Orioles)	3	3	0	0	0	1	0	11
Early Wynn (Indians)	0.1	3	2	2	0	0	0	4
Billy Pierce* (White Sox)	1.2	2	3	3	2	3	0	9
Don Mossi (Indians)	0.2	1	0	0	0	1	0	2
Bob Grim (Yankees)	0.1	0	0	0	0	0	0	1
Totals	9	9	5	5	2	6	0	36

National League	IP	H	R	ER	BB	SO	HR	BF
Curt Simmons* (Phillies) L	1	2	2	2	2	0	0	7
Lew Burdette (Braves)	4	2	0	0	1	0	0	15
Jack Sanford (Phillies)	1	2	1	1	0	0	0	5
Larry Jackson (Cardinals)	2	1	0	0	1	0	0	8
Clem Labine (Dodgers)	1	3	3	1	0	1	0	7
Totals	9	10	6	4	4	1	0	42

* Simmons faced four batters in second.

* Pierce faced four batters in ninth.

a-Singled for Bunning in fourth. b-Hit into force play for Hoak in fifth. c-Hit into double play for McMillan in fifth. d-Grounded out for Sanford in sixth. e-Flied out for Temple in sixth. f-Doubled for Robinson in seventh. g-Struck out for Jackson in eighth. h-Singled for Bailey in ninth. i-Flied out for Labine in ninth. E: Schoendienst. DP: AL, Malzone-Fox-Skowron. LOB: American 9, National 4. 2B: Musial, Skowron, Bell, Minoso. 3B: Mays. SF: Fox. WP: Sanford, Pierce. Umpires: Changed positions in fifth to: HP - Johnny Stevens, 1B - Hal Dixon, 2B - Larry Napp, 3B - Frank Dascoli, LF - Stan Landes, RF - Nestor Chylak. Time: 2:43. Attendance: 30,693.

★LOCAL ANGLE★

The former Sportsman's Park
played All-Star host as
reborn "Busch Stadium."

From the scene at the ballpark to the buzz around town, St. Louis' host-city role helped define the 1957 All-Star experience.

Scrubby Dutch splendor

The '57 All-Star Game marked the first appearance of St. Louis' ballpark on the big national stage since the Cardinals had bought the facility from the St. Louis Browns in April 1953 – a transaction that occurred less than two months after Anheuser-Busch Inc. had purchased the Redbirds franchise from Fred M. Saigh Jr. Upon assuming control of the park, the new Cardinals ownership, led by August A. Busch Jr., had planned to rename it Budweiser Stadium, but quickly did an about-face and decided on "Busch."

American Leaguers, who hadn't been back to the ballpark since the Browns bolted to Baltimore after the '53 season, were impressed with what they saw. "Gosh, it looks as though it was freshly painted just for this occasion," one junior-circuit player said. "It's hard for me to believe I'm in old Sportsman's Park. It looks so different. Gussie Busch is surely a handy man with a paintbrush."

For his part, Busch reportedly was at the park before 9 a.m. on game day to personally inspect every lavatory, concession stand and dressing room to ensure the facility gleamed with perfection.

The stadium became the first to play host to three Midsummer Classics.

Resident All-Stars

The Cardinals landed four players on the 1957 N.L. All-Star roster: Stan Musial, Wally Moon, Larry Jackson and Hal Smith. Musial came from behind in the fans' voting to outpoll Cincinnati's George Crowe by more than 90,000 votes and nab the starting first-base job; he was the only non-Redlegs player voted into the starting lineup by fans, due to the voting shenanigans in Cincinnati.

Musial's three fellow Redbirds were added to the National League roster by manager Walter Alston of Brooklyn. Moon finished second to the Redlegs' Frank Robinson in the vote for left fielder, and Smith was runner-up to Cincy's Ed Bailey at catcher. Both were a distant second, however, with the crush of ballots from Cincinnati leaving both Cardinals about 700,000 votes in arrears.

One other Redbird, shortstop Al Dark, was No. 2 in voting at his position, but he was overlooked by Alston as an N.L. reserve. Dark trailed Cincy shortstop Roy McMillan by more than a half-million votes.

★ **1957 ALL-STAR GAME** ★

With the All-Star Game hitting its stride as a must-see exhibition, fans turned sidewalks into staging lanes hours before Busch's gates opened.

Two Cardinals also took on pregame roles for the N.L. team. Veteran righthander Herm Wehmeier served as one of the batting-practice pitchers (the Cubs' Dick Littlefield was the other), and reserve catcher Hobie Landrith was behind the plate for B.P.

More acclaim for the game

The *St. Louis Globe-Democrat* reported how a cab driver seemed to nail the prevailing atmosphere in St. Louis. "It's like the whole city just woke up the last three weeks," the cabbie said. "It's this baseball. It's like the city put on a new cloak or something."

The red-hot Redbirds' surge from sixth to first place in the six weeks preceding the All-Star Game had played a big role in generating baseball excitement throughout the city, but the Midsummer Classic itself had come a long way, evolving into a must-see event. Musial noted that the "All-Star Game means a lot more today than it did when I first started playing in it. It used to be that some of the fellows would beg off, on any kind of excuse, but now the players are taking it seriously because it

means so much more to them, with the pension fund getting a lot of money from it."

The game's importance didn't stop the St. Louis slugger from savoring the special nature of the day – he was seen shooting movies of his teammates near the end of pregame drills.

Mother Nature cooperates

The weather outlook for the day was pure St. Louis: hot and humid with scattered thundershowers. Game time was set for 1:30 p.m., but in the event rain were to wipe out the afternoon's proceedings, officials planned to reschedule the contest for 8 p.m.

Rain did fall overnight and skies were overcast early on game day, but the sun broke through and the weather, in the words of a visiting columnist, "was delightful thereafter."

Seeing Red again

Red Schoendienst, dealt by the Cards to the Giants in a shocking move 13 months earlier, was now in Milwaukee flannels as an N.L. reserve after figuring in a June trade-deadline swap for the second consecutive year.

Schoendienst popped into his old Cardinals clubhouse and asked trainer Bob Bauman for the "hitting pills" that a former Redbirds farmhand, now in the pharmaceutical business, had supplied the St. Louis club. The pills, the whimsical story went, helped fuel the Cards' turnaround that season. As proof positive this was baseball in the 1950s and not circa 2009, the dandy little tablets were vitamin-C pills.

As it turned out, what Red really needed was something to steady his reflexes. His costly ninth-inning fumble of a ground ball – he was usually surehanded in the field – was the only error of the game. And on his way out of town, *The Sporting News* reported, he was issued a speeding ticket while driving to Union Station to catch a train.

Worth the price

The crowd of 30,693 paid $122,027 to get into Sportsman's Park, netting baseball $104,349.62 in gate receipts, which

Cardinals broadcasters Joe Garagiola (left) and Harry Caray (right) accepted commemorative gold records from KMOX Radio general manager Robert Hyland in advance of their radio broadcast of the '57 Dream Game.

★ 1957 ALL-STAR GAME ★

Three St. Louisans graced the American League's All-Star cast, (from left) Yogi Berra, Elston Howard and Roy Sievers.

went to the pension fund.

Ted Williams didn't wait long to give the paying customers what they wanted to see, knocking the first pitch he was served in batting practice over the right-field pavilion roof. For all the hype surrounding the Williams-Musial showdown, the principals seemed more interested in camaraderie than rivalry. *The Sporting News* reported the two sluggers watched one another during B.P., and each expressed ample praise for his "adversary."

"You have to like Ted," commented the Cardinals first baseman. "He never swings wildly and always seems to know what he's doing."

Faces in the crowd

Jacqueline James, performing in "Guys and Dolls" at the outdoor Muny theater in the city's Forest Park, gave a stirring rendition of the national anthem as the cry of "play ball!" neared.

Cards manager Fred Hutchinson and the Redbirds' McDaniel brothers rubbed elbows with fans while watching the action unfold from seats behind the N.L. dugout. They were joined by Lindy and Von's parents, who had come to St. Louis to catch the just-concluded Cards-Redlegs action.

Commissioner Ford Frick settled into a seat next to the screen in the temporary boxes set up on the field, so he'd be easily accessible to umpires if a question arose during the game.

Almost full coverage

Harry Caray and Joe Garagiola, the Cardinals' leading men behind the mike, and Cleveland's Bob Neal handled the national radio broadcast of the game on NBC. Jack Buck, the third man in the Cards' booth, was in his fourth year with the club and not involved in the nationwide coverage.

Meanwhile, KSD-TV cameras originated the telecast for NBC-TV. However, viewers missed one of the game's key plays, when Gus Bell tried to race from first to third base in the ninth inning. Cameras had been focused on Ernie Banks' ground-ball smash into short left field, then panned to the Pirates' Hank Foiles as he scored. When the cameras finally cut to third, all viewers saw was the umpire gesturing that Bell was out, as the Reds outfielder got to his feet.

Homecoming report

Yankees catcher Yogi Berra, pride of The Hill, played the entire game – he'd been an A.L. reserve in the 1948 contest at Sportsman's Park but didn't get into the action – and drove in the Americans' third run. It was his first RBI in nine All-Star appearances.

Two other native St. Louisans weren't so fortunate. The Yankees' Elston Howard and the Senators' Roy Sievers remained on the bench throughout. Howard, a third-year major leaguer, seemed OK with his fate, but the inactivity was tough for the veteran Sievers, who was sitting on 20 homers and would finish the season with an A.L.-leading 42.

"I guess my biggest disappointment was in disappointing my hometown folks," Sievers said. "My mother, my dad and all my friends were there." Sievers said A.L. manager Casey Stengel had intended to employ him as a pinch hitter for pitcher Billy Pierce to lead off the ninth inning "but then Billy was going so good that Casey left him in there."

Hometown scorecard

Musial's fourth-inning double off the right-field pavilion's screen provided one of the day's highlights for the local citizenry. As for the rest of the Redbirds, Jackson was busiest with two innings of scoreless relief in his first-ever All-Star role. Moon, appointed to his first N.L. All-Star squad, grounded out in a pinch-hitting appearance. Smith, marking his second season in the majors, remained on the bench.

– Joe Hoppel

★ **1957 ALL-STAR GAME** ★

YOUR STARTER AND YOUR CLOSER.

From the first pitch to the last out, the refreshing taste of Bud Light won't fill you up and never lets you down. Bud Light. **THE DIFFERENCE IS DRINKABILITY.**

Problems at the polls

It was the ultimate "get out the vote" campaign, with bold comments and suggestions printed right on the ballot. "VOTE OFTEN – VOTE EARLY" screamed one message. "Fill out any number of ballots" advised another.

Such was All-Star Game voting, Cincinnati-style, as conducted in 1957 by the city's *Times-Star* newspaper, which had been designated the area's official All-Star polling organization. The *Times-Star* knew most of its readers would vote for worthy Redlegs players, but its methods virtually assured they'd vote for even those not so deserving.

The newspaper's All-Star ballot listed the name of each Redlegs starter alongside the space allotted for filling in the name of a National League starting position player – in those days, voting selections were handwritten and ballots were mailed in or dropped off at a grocery store or neighborhood watering hole. Not surprisingly, the paper's crib sheet for picking the N.L.'s eight starters (the pitcher was not included in voting) was spelled out under the heading of "Let's Back the Redlegs!"

An estimated 350,000 ballots were distributed to area taverns by the Burger Brewing Co., which sponsored Reds broadcasts. One bartender cited a young girl who picked up 1,400 ballots, took them home, and returned them properly filled out and signed.

The result of all this finagling and cheerleading: Seven Reds cruised to victory because of a monstrous volume of votes from southern Ohio.

Commissioner Ford Frick allowed five of the vote-winning Redlegs – second baseman Johnny Temple, shortstop Roy McMillan, third baseman Don Hoak, catcher Ed Bailey and left fielder Frank Robinson – to retain their starter status, but he dictated that two other winners, right fielder Wally Post and center fielder Gus Bell, would not. Post would give way to the Braves' Hank Aaron and Bell would be replaced by the Giants' Willie Mays.

The geniuses in Cincinnati had chosen Post, who was hitting a paltry .231 at the All-Star break with 11 homers and 46 runs batted in, over Aaron, who entered the Dream Game with

In 1957, the Nationals' starting outfielders had a combined nine All-Star selections; by the end of their careers, (from left) Frank Robinson, Hank Aaron and Willie Mays totaled 63.

★ 1957 ALL-STAR GAME ★

LET'S BACK THE REDLEGS!
CINCINNATI TIMES-STAR
ALL-STAR BALLOT

NATIONAL LEAGUE

Your choices must be written in blank spaces.

---------------------------------- 1st B.

---------------------------------- 2nd B.

---------------------------------- 3rd B.

---------------------------------- S. S.

---------------------------------- L. F.

---------------------------------- C. F.

---------------------------------- R. F.

---------------------------------- C.

HERE ARE YOUR REDLEGS

1st Base
CROWE

2nd Base
TEMPLE

3rd Base
HOAK

Short Stop
McMILLAN

Left Field
ROBINSON

Center Field
BELL

Right Field
POST

Catcher
BAILEY

(Pitchers will be picked by managers)
Fill out any number of ballots and mail to:
All-Star, Times-Star, P. O. Box 1399, Cincinnati 99, Ohio,
or deposit in Kroger Kwiz Box at any Kroger
Supermarket, or deposit at your favorite tavern.

Name ....

Address ....

City ....

VOTE OFTEN — VOTE EARLY

All ballots must be received at TIMES-STAR
before noon, Wed., June 26.

COUPON WILL RUN DAILY

Baseball Commissioner Ford Frick has designated the TIMES-STAR as the official All-Star Game Poll newspaper in this area.

Little was left to the imagination of Cincinnati voters, who fulfilled their mission by voting seven "Redlegs" to berths in the starting lineup.

league-leading figures in batting average (.347), home runs (27) and RBIs (73). Cincinnatians also had preferred Bell (eight homers, 41 RBIs and a .291 mark) over Mays (13 homers, 48 RBIs and a .307 average).

First baseman George Crowe, one of Cincinnati's top statistical performers (.305 average with 18 homers and 55 RBIs over the first half), didn't make the N.L. team as a starter or reserve. After he, too, was ruled out as a starter by Frick and replaced by Stan Musial – the Cincy slugger was outpolling Musial at the time – Crowe was bypassed as a roster addition by N.L. manager Walter Alston of Brooklyn, who picked his own man, Gil Hodges, as the reserve first baseman. Hodges was hitting .309 at the break, with 10 homers and 38 RBIs.

It turned out that Musial didn't need to be anointed by the commissioner, thank you very much. He rallied to win the fan vote, an honor that befitted his .341 average, 20 homers and 66 RBIs.

Alston included Bell – but skipped over Post – when he completed his roster, giving Cincinnati six players on the Nationals' squad, an N.L. total matched only by Milwaukee. The Redlegs' Robinson was the top vote-getter in both leagues, with a tally of 745,689.

Crowe and Post did receive a consolation prize, in the form of an All-Star Game memento from the N.L. office in recognition of the huge popular vote they'd garnered.

Red Scare reaction

The Cincinnati Redlegs? Say what? The "Redlegs" moniker was first adopted – but seldom used – by the Cincinnati club earlier in the '50s, when "Reds" had all kinds of negative political overtones. In 1956, the tweaked nickname seemed to gain legs when the familiar emblem of a wishbone-C with "Reds" therein was dropped from the uniform jersey in favor a lone, unembellished C. The revised uniform lasted five seasons, even though "Redlegs" seemed to lose favor among fans and media long before then.

Lots of Yankees, little controversy

There was no ballot overload for the Americans' star squad, which suited Frick just fine. Fans voted two Yankees (Mickey Mantle and Yogi Berra), two Tigers (Al Kaline and Harvey Kuenn) and one player each from Boston (Ted Williams, the A.L. leader in votes), Chicago (Nellie Fox), Cleveland (Vic Wertz) and Baltimore (George Kell) to the Americans' starting lineup. A.L. manager Casey Stengel of the Yankees made it three starters for Detroit when he selected Jim Bunning to open on the mound.

The Yankees' cast on the A.L. team swelled to eight when Stengel added pinstriped pitchers Bob Grim and Bobby Shantz, outfielder-catcher Elston Howard, first baseman Bill Skowron, shortstop Gil McDougald and second baseman Bobby Richardson. The Tigers boasted the next-best A.L. representation with four players, landing outfielder Charley Maxwell as a reserve.

Mantle, a Triple Crown winner in 1956, was leading the A.L. in hitting at the break with a .369 average (26 points ahead of Williams) and also was tops in homers with 22. He was third in RBIs with 57, only three behind teammate Skowron.

Stengel criticized the ballot-box stuffing in Cincinnati, but he also emphasized that A.L. starters Kuenn, Kell and Wertz "shouldn't have been picked because they're not having good

His presence was bemoaned by his All-Star manager, but Cleveland's Vic Wertz knocked in the game's first run with a second-inning single to left field.

years." Yet no starter on either team was going as poorly – at least in terms of batting average – as Berra, his own Yankees catcher. Yogi entered the game with a .232 average, although he did have 12 homers and 42 RBIs.

Missouri's other major league team, the Kansas City Athletics, had only one player on the A.L. roster: shortstop Joe DeMaestri, who

didn't get into the game. The A's had two other players on hand, though: pitchers Alex Kellner and Wally Burnette, who threw batting practice for the Americans.

Coaches corner

Yankees aides Frank Crosetti and Jim Turner handled All-Star coaching duties for the A.L., while Cubs rookie manager Bob Scheffing and Pirates sophomore field boss Bobby Bragan got the assignment for the N.L.

Parting gifts

In addition to the traditional mementos doled out to players on both teams – watches, rings, candelabra and punch bowls were among the items they could choose from – each member of the A.L. squad was given two baseballs to be autographed by his teammates as souvenirs. Most of the younger players, though, cajoled Crosetti, who was in charge of handing out the mementos, into giving them extra balls.

Perhaps the most unexpected gift came from the state of Idaho, in honor of Cardinals pitcher Larry Jackson, its native son. Each All-Star was to receive a 25-pound gift box of U.S. Idaho gem potatoes in the fall, after the crop of spuds had been harvested.

Old Zachariah

Missouri native and longtime Dodgers standout Zack Wheat, whose big-league career had ended three decades earlier, attended

A participant in St. Louis' first three All-Star Games, Ted Williams was the pregame center of attention, for fans and N.L.-president-turned-commissioner Ford Frick (right).

Fox and Kaline – the entire game, got his unwanted trio of Kuenn, Kell and Wertz out of the game almost as quickly as he could (the middle of the fourth inning) to beef up his lineup and employed three pitchers in a dicey ninth inning.

Alston played Musial, Aaron and Mays throughout, pulled starting pitcher Curt Simmons (Phillies) before he retired a batter in the second inning, and kept highly effective righthander Lew Burdette in the game for four innings – a stint in which the Braves hurler pitched two-hit ball (the Milwaukee standout was able to exceed the ordained three-inning All-Star limit because he had not begun the inning in which he entered the game). Also, not a single player on either team withdrew from the game because of injury, feigned or otherwise.

Though the National League was now getting the hang of this All-Star thing, the A.L. held on for its 14th victory against 10 losses.

Oh, for the '57 model Minoso

All-Star Game standout Minnie Minoso, who wound up with impressive numbers (.310 average, 96 runs and 103 RBIs) for a second-place White Sox club, would call Busch Stadium home five years later. His memories of this day in St. Louis in '57, though, would far outweigh those of an entire season as a Cardinal in 1962. Beset with injuries after being acquired from the White Sox for Joe Cunningham in November 1961, Minnie appeared in only 39 games for the Cards. He batted .196 and was sold to the Senators before the start of the next season.

Post-break wrapup

Williams, who turned 39 in August, was the No. 1 individual headliner in the second half of the season. He hit an unfathomable .453 after the break, finished with a .388 average and won his fifth A.L. batting crown. Mantle's hopes for a repeat Triple Crown died when his power numbers dropped off and Williams went on his tear. Still, Mick hit a resounding .365.

The Braves were the big story, team-wise, rewarding Milwaukee's rabid fan base with a World Series title in the club's fifth season after its transfer from Boston.

The real blockbuster, though, was the news that the Brooklyn Dodgers and New York Giants – after months of negotiations – would relocate to the West Coast for the start of the 1958 season. The shifts of the storied franchises to Los Angeles and San Francisco, which reflected the nation's ever-evolving demographics, marked a sea change in baseball's geographic and financial structure.

Oh, yes, there was one other item of major interest: Fans would be disenfranchised the next time All-Star Game voting rolled around. They had chosen the starting lineups (excluding pitchers) for 11 consecutive years, but the commissioner's office – reacting to the antics in Cincinnati – turned over the vote to managers, coaches and players in 1958 and didn't return it to the fans until 1970.

– *Joe Hoppel*

Mighty as an All-Star, Minnie was middling as a Cardinal, suffering through an injury-plagued '62 season.

---

the game. The Red Sox's Ted Williams made a point of seeking him out, telling Wheat he was well aware of the old outfielder's reputation for hitting "nothing but line drives." Williams also offered that if voters "wake up now, they'll get you in that Hall (of Fame), where you belong." Two years later, Wheat was Cooperstown-bound.

Williams was the lone All-Star present who had played in St. Louis' first Dream Game in 1940. A second-year major leaguer at the time, he went 0-for-2 in that game as the Americans' starting left fielder. Injury limited Williams to a pinch-hitting appearance in the 1948 classic at St. Louis.

Playing to win

As the game unfolded, it was strikingly clear how badly both sides wanted to win. Stengel used four players – Mantle, Berra,

Already abuzz with excitement over the Cardinals' resurgence, the North Side neighborhood around Busch Stadium had a block-party aura on an All-Star Tuesday afternoon.

Pennant fever and Von Mania. They gripped St. Louis when the All-Star Game came to town in 1957, creating a frenzied setting that few All-Star venues have experienced in the long history of baseball's Midsummer Classic.

The Cardinals, fourth-place finishers with a sub-.500 record in 1956, had bolted to the top of the National League standings – and done so with a flourish. In a doubleheader that sent them into the All-Star break at exactly the midpoint of the 154-game schedule, the Cards swept Cincinnati before their largest home crowd of the season. The victories pushed St. Louis' winning streak to five and gave the club nine wins in its last 10 games.

The twin-bill throng of 30,516 came to watch a red-hot team

that stoked hope for the franchise's first N.L. flag in 11 years. Among the fans' favorites: the incomparable Stan Musial and the budding sensation Ken Boyer; pepperpot second baseman Don Blasingame; sizzling Joe Cunningham, who didn't disappoint with a six-hit day in the doubleheader that raised the part-time player's batting average to .391; sweet-swinging outfielder Wally Moon, who crushed his 15th home run of the young season in the nightcap; outfielder Del Ennis, a big-time run producer who had been obtained in the offseason from the Phillies; and pitching mainstays Larry Jackson, Lindy McDaniel, Vinegar Bend Mizell and Sam (Toothpick) Jones.

Most of all, though, fans clamored to see 18-year-old hurler Von McDaniel, a $50,000 signee who had burst upon the scene less than a month earlier. In his jump from the Oklahoma high school ranks to the Cardinals (at the time, big-bucks "bonus babies" were required to take a roster spot), the righthander broke in with two scintillating relief appearances on the road – both four-inning, one-hit performances – against the Phillies and Dodgers.

In the game at Brooklyn, Cards shortstop Al Dark went to the mound to confer with Von as Dodgers star Duke Snider strode to the plate. "You know who this is, Von?" asked Dark, wanting to make certain the kid pitched carefully to the man who was on his way to a fifth consecutive 40-homer season. "Oh sure," McDaniel responded. "Mr. Snider." With St. Louis ahead by one run in the seventh inning, the phenom proceeded to strike out the Duke of Flatbush.

In his first major league start, McDaniel tossed a two-hit shutout against the Dodgers before a home crowd of 27,972. Von, the brother of 21-year-old Cards starter Lindy, took a 4-0 record and 1.71 ERA into the pre-classic double-dip against Cincinnati. With the crowd roaring its approval, Von yielded two runs over seven innings in a game St. Louis won in 10 innings.

As the All-Stars gathered in St. Louis for the July 9 Dream Game, the first-place Cards were 46-31 and 2½ games in front of Milwaukee.

Strange as it seems, the Redbirds' season appears to have been jump-started by the decision to move Boyer out of his third-base slot – he would go on to win five Gold Gloves at that position – and into center field in place of slumping first-year player Bobby Gene Smith. In turn, the club inserted rookie Eddie Kasko at the hot corner. The switch was made on May 23, the night the club fell into sixth place; by June 20, the Cards were atop the league after a 21-7 run.

At the time of Boyer's exit from third, the *St. Louis Post-Dispatch* reported "his fielding has been a steady threat to Cardinal pitchers' sanity." For his part, Kasko played well defensively and proved solid with the bat.

Musial had his usual locked-in look at the plate – he was in a fierce fight with the Braves' Hank Aaron and the Pirates' Dee Fondy for the N.L. batting title – but proved he was a quintessential lunch-bucket guy, too. Four weeks before the All-Star Game, Stan set an N.L. record by playing in his 823rd consecutive game. The mark had been held by 1930s Pittsburgh first baseman Gus Suhr.

Moon, known more for his all-around hitting skills than for the power he was exhibiting over the first half of the year, hit safely in 24 straight games beginning May 5. It turned out to be the majors' longest streak in '57.

Teenage rookie sensation Von McDaniel helped pitch the Cardinals into first place at the All-Star break.

★ 1957 ALL-STAR GAME ★

A year earlier, Musial modeled a fashion faux pas destined for infamy.

Not only did the Cardinals have the look of a potential winner, they had their old-time sartorial look, as well – a fact that absolutely delighted the Redbird faithful. New general manager Frank Lane had stripped the traditional birds-on-the-bat design from the front of the team's uniforms in 1956; a plain-script "Cardinals" was used, along with a bird-in-a-batting-stance emblem on the sleeve.

"I didn't realize the tradition of the birds on the uniform meant so much to St. Louis fans," the clueless Lane said after restoring the time-honored motif for the '57 season.

Down the stretch

The Cardinals lost seven of their first nine games after the break but rebounded with a 14-2 tear entering August. Just as abruptly, a nine-game losing streak that commenced Aug. 6 dropped the Redbirds out of first place for good, and Milwaukee clinched the pennant against the Cardinals on Sept. 23, when Hank Aaron hit a game-winning, two-run homer in the 11th inning. St. Louis finished in second place at 87-67, eight games back.

Von McDaniel experienced more downs than ups in the second act of his big-league debut. After being roughed up in his first two post-All-Star starts, he set baseball on its ear again on July 28 by pitching a one-hitter against the Pirates. But he had a shaky end to the season, failing to last even two innings in each of his last two starts. He finished the year 7-5 with a 3.22 ERA.

Von's flameout came quickly. He developed arm trouble in 1958, pitched in only two games that year and was done as a major leaguer at age 19.

Musial injured his shoulder at Philadelphia on Aug. 22 and left the game; his consecutive-games playing streak ended the next night when he sat out against the Phils. Or had it been stopped a month earlier?

Oddly, the length of his streak was still in limbo because the Cardinals had yet to complete a July 21 game that had been suspended in the ninth inning – a game in which Stan the Man had not appeared. Though Musial was still hurting when the July 21 contest (against the Pirates) was completed on Aug. 27, the Cards got him into the game in the ninth as a pinch-runner and defensive replacement. The appearance enabled Musial's streak to end at 895 games, not 862.

The time on the bench didn't stop Musial from winning his seventh, and last, N.L. batting title, hitting .351. He wasn't the only Cardinal to put up laudable numbers. Ennis led the club in RBIs with 105, Moon wound up with a career-high 24 home runs and Cunningham hit .318 in 261 at-bats. Jackson and Lindy McDaniel were both 15-game winners.

A championship year in St. Louis? No. A memorable season? Absolutely.

– Joe Hoppel

Wally Moon cracked a career-best 24 homers in his only All-Star season as a Cardinal.

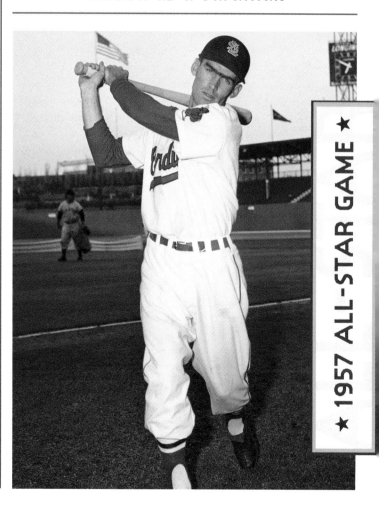

★ 1957 ALL-STAR GAME ★

★ 1966 ALL-STAR GAME ★

NATIONAL LEAGUE 2, AMERICAN LEAGUE 1

BUSCH MEMORIAL STADIUM, JULY 12

official program

1966 all-star game

★GAME STORY★

By JOE HOPPEL

Under a broiling sun, the 1966 National League All-Stars plate their first run at brand-new Busch Memorial Stadium.

St. Louis baseball staples — tight defense, stingy pitching and scorching heat — define a 2-1, 10-inning victory by the National League.

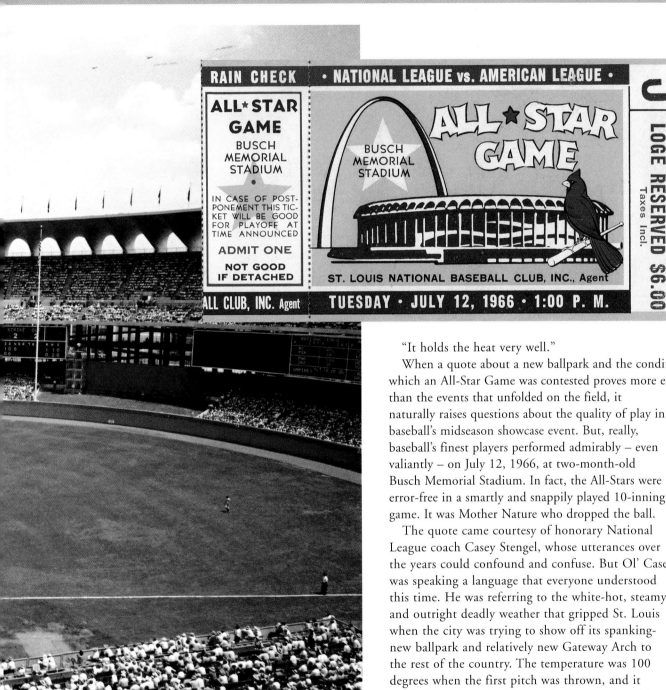

RAIN CHECK • NATIONAL LEAGUE vs. AMERICAN LEAGUE •

ALL★STAR GAME

BUSCH MEMORIAL STADIUM

IN CASE OF POST-PONEMENT THIS TIC-KET WILL BE GOOD FOR PLAYOFF AT TIME ANNOUNCED

ADMIT ONE

NOT GOOD IF DETACHED

ALL CLUB, INC. Agent

BUSCH MEMORIAL STADIUM

ALL★STAR GAME

ST. LOUIS NATIONAL BASEBALL CLUB, INC., Agent

TUESDAY • JULY 12, 1966 • 1:00 P. M.

ENTER GATE 3

SEC. 236

ROW 20

SEAT 10

LOGE RESERVED $6.00

Taxes Incl.

"It holds the heat very well."

When a quote about a new ballpark and the conditions in which an All-Star Game was contested proves more enduring than the events that unfolded on the field, it naturally raises questions about the quality of play in baseball's midseason showcase event. But, really, baseball's finest players performed admirably – even valiantly – on July 12, 1966, at two-month-old Busch Memorial Stadium. In fact, the All-Stars were error-free in a smartly and snappily played 10-inning game. It was Mother Nature who dropped the ball.

The quote came courtesy of honorary National League coach Casey Stengel, whose utterances over the years could confound and confuse. But Ol' Case was speaking a language that everyone understood this time. He was referring to the white-hot, steamy and outright deadly weather that gripped St. Louis when the city was trying to show off its spanking-new ballpark and relatively new Gateway Arch to the rest of the country. The temperature was 100 degrees when the first pitch was thrown, and it reached 104 later in the game before topping off at 105 shortly after its conclusion.

And for those who maintained that the high, circular design of the gleaming downtown stadium was anything but ventilation-friendly, there's this question: Exactly what kind of facility – other than some newfangled indoor arena, like the air-conditioned Astrodome

★ 1966 ALL-STAR GAME ★

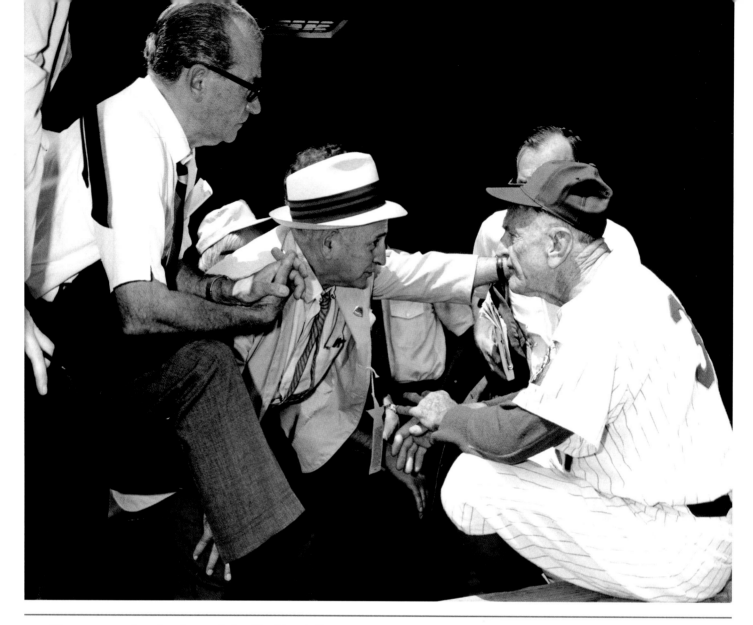

Two weeks before his Hall of Fame induction, honorary N.L. coach Casey Stengel delivered an observation for the ages when scribes quizzed him about St. Louis' new summer playpen.

that had opened a year earlier – could have made things more tolerable?

Stengel's remark was among the few lighthearted comments anyone could come up with about the weather. Two American League starters, center fielder Al Kaline and third baseman Brooks Robinson, were among those weighing in on the serious side.

"I was the hottest I've ever been," said the Tigers' Kaline, known as one of baseball's true gamers. "I got so dizzy that I had to ask to be replaced."

"I used to think it was hot in Little Rock," said the Orioles' Robinson, a native of Arkansas, "but this was the worst ever. It seemed like 200 degrees under that batting helmet. You could feel your brains frying."

As hot as it was for the players on the floor of the stadium –

fortunately, the park didn't have the almost-combustible AstroTurf surface in its early years – the All-Stars could at least escape to the dugout or a runway to dodge the broiling sun when not at their defensive positions or involved offensively. Fans had no such readily available refuge. Many customers fled the high-priced field-box seats – and other unprotected vantage points – for at least temporary relief in the concession-area concourses. Others left the ballpark early. And, according to the *St. Louis Globe-Democrat*, more than 125 fans were forced to make their way to first-aid stations, some on stretchers.

Those members of the 49,936-person crowd who were able to stick with the game were not disappointed by what they witnessed. Oh, some might have preferred more offense, yet no one really expected a high-scoring contest in the spacious new stadium, whose size was compounded by the fact that the ball didn't carry well within its confines. In the 29 games played at new Busch since its opening on May 12, St. Louis opponents had scored two or fewer runs 21 times and the Cardinals had been shut out or limited to one run on 12 occasions.

Plus, the nine N.L. and A.L. players who had whacked 20 or more home runs by the break were going up against a strange bit of St. Louis All-Star history: Even at cozy Sportsman's Park/old Busch, a total of only three homers had been struck in the All-Star Games of 1940, 1948 and 1957.

Of course, if the "good pitching beats good hitting" theory held true, run production figured to be meager, regardless of venue. Four members of the Nationals' eight-man staff had sub-2.00 earned-run averages, and the rest had figures ranging from 2.04 to 2.73. The Americans' pitching wasn't quite as parsimonious, but seven of the eight A.L. hurlers boasted ERAs from 1.89 to 3.23.

And consider the starters for the 37th All-Star Game: Dodgers lefthander Sandy Koufax, who was 15-4 with a 1.61 ERA at the break and had pitched no-hitters in each of the four previous seasons, and fast-emerging Tigers righthander Denny McLain, who at age 22 was zeroed in with a 13-4

record and had won 30 of his last 40 decisions.

Koufax and McLain were nearly as torrid as the weather in their three-inning stints; Koufax allowed only one baserunner and McLain retired all nine batters he faced. Koufax paid for letting one man aboard – his wild pitch eventually enabled that runner to score – but the lights-out hurler with the arthritic elbow deserved better.

After retiring the Twins' Tony Oliva on a fly ball to start the second inning, Koufax yielded a line-drive hit to Robinson, whose smash to left field was misplayed by the Braves' Hank Aaron. Robinson should have been perched on first base with a single, but the painfully slow Oriole legged it all the way to third when the ball skipped past Aaron, who apparently lost the ball in the white shirts in the stands and then attempted to make a shoestring catch. Red Sox rookie George Scott fouled out, but with Detroit's Bill Freehan at the plate, Koufax sailed a pitch past catcher Joe Torre (Braves) and Robinson ambled home.

Sandy later acknowledged that he was struggling a bit, an admission that must have startled mere mortals when they checked out his one-hit-over-three-frames pitching line. "I

Two months after its inaugural game, Busch welcomed the rest of baseball for the only All-Star gala staged at the ballpark during its 40-year history.

★ 1966 ALL-STAR GAME ★

First-time All-Star Denny McLain dispatched the Nationals with a 28-pitch, three-inning masterpiece.

Alston selected the Phillies' Jim Bunning, who had pitched so brilliantly as an American Leaguer in the '57 All-Star Game at Grand and Dodier, to succeed his Dodgers meal ticket.

Kaat encountered immediate trouble. Mays, who had compiled a .389 batting average and collected a record 21 hits in his 16 previous All-Star Games, began the N.L. fourth

wish that I had McLain's curveball. I haven't had one for two weeks," lamented Koufax, who had been rocked for three home runs in his last start before the break. "The wild pitch (that scored Brooks Robinson) was a curve. And I tried three or four others, but no dice."

McLain, conversely, was on a roll with his repertoire. He needed only 28 pitches to subdue the Nationals over three innings, boosting A.L. hopes that the junior circuit could end a three-game losing streak in All-Star Game competition, which it had long dominated. On his way to a 20-victory season and two years away from ringing up 31 wins, McLain sneaked called third strikes past mashers Willie Mays (Giants) and Aaron in the first inning and struck out Torre in the second.

The Tigers hurler completed his stint by facing the Cardinals' Curt Flood, whose appearance as a pinch-hitter for Koufax in the third inning gave sweltering St. Louis fans reason to come to their feet for something other than a dash to the nearest overhang or water fountain. The cheers subsided, though, when Flood hit a grounder that bounded off McLain and caromed to second baseman Bobby Knoop (Angels), who threw out the speedy Redbird.

A.L. manager Sam Mele of the Twins went with his own staff ace, Jim Kaat, to follow McLain. N.L. skipper Walter

Part of a daunting N.L. staff, Juan Marichal kept the Americans off the scoreboard in innings six through eight.

Brooks Robinson, named the game's MVP, opted for ice water over champagne on a day "you could feel your brains frying."

with a single to left off the Minnesota lefthander. Pittsburgh's Roberto Clemente followed with a single to center that moved Mays to second, and after Aaron fouled out, Willie scooted to third on a forceout grounder by Willie McCovey (Giants). The Cubs' Ron Santo then reached on an infield hit, tapping a dribbler down the third-base line that scored Mays and extended the Say Hey Kid's All-Star record for runs scored to 19.

Pitching and defense, which already had dazzled the crowd, proceeded to take a toehold in the 1-1 game. Kaat, the Yankees' Mel Stottlemyre and the Indians' Sonny Siebert blanked the N.L. squad from the fifth inning through the ninth. Hot-corner wizard Robinson, who had made a great play by snaring Santo's sizzling liner in the second inning, bolted to the bag to dig out Aaron's sharply hit grounder in the sixth and again flashed to his right in the ninth to come up with Santo's ground ball over the bag. Brooks' arm nailed both frustrated hitters at first base.

Bunning and the San Francisco duo of Juan Marichal and Gaylord Perry were firing zeroes, too,

★ 1966 ALL-STAR GAME ★

Dodgers shortstop Maury Wills, peeved over not starting, punched a game-winning single into right-center in his first plate appearance.

bringing about something that not even the most zealous of baseball fans really wanted on this scorcher of a day: an extra-inning game.

Robinson, who had been scorching hot in his own right with his bat and glove and would be named the game's MVP, opened the A.L. 10th with a pop-fly single (his third hit) and took second on a wild pitch by Perry. After Norm Cash (Tigers) flied out and Earl Battey (Twins) walked, the Yankees' Bobby Richardson lofted a foul pop that seemed destined to fall out of play down the first-base line. But N.L. first baseman McCovey, known as Stretch, lived up to his nickname and reached far into the stands to make the catch, denying further life at the plate for the pesky Richardson. Perry then struck out the Angels' Jim Fregosi.

Senators southpaw Pete Richert entered the game in the bottom half of the inning – a pressure-packed situation under any circumstances but additionally unnerving on this day

because of who and what greeted him: Cardinals catcher Tim McCarver was standing at the plate, with the St. Louis partisans loudly urging him on, and the scoreboard was flashing a message about how former Redbird favorites Red Schoendienst and Stan Musial had won All-Star Games (Red in 1950, Stan in 1955) with extra-innings home runs.

McCarver didn't park one into the seats, but he did single into the hole between first and second. The Mets' Ron Hunt sacrificed him to second, which brought up the Dodgers' Maury Wills, an unhappy camper because he hadn't started the game or even gotten into the fray until the eighth (when, like McCarver, he entered as a defensive replacement). Wills, who had quickly made an impact in the tight game with a back-to-the-plate catch of a pop fly by Baltimore's Frank Robinson in the Americans' ninth, faked a bunt. But the expert bat handler then swung away and stroked the ball safely into right-center, and the National League and the sun-baked, pro-N.L. crowd

Scoring from second on Wills' hit, Cardinal Tim McCarver got a winner's welcome from Giants Gaylord Perry and Willie Mays and N.L. skipper Walter Alston.

Classic National League know-how — situational hitting and aggressive baserunning — by the McCarver-Wills-Alston triumvirate gave the N.L. a 2-1 victory and a 19-17-1 record in All-Star play.

seemed to have it made in the shade — figuratively in the sense of the game's outcome and literally in terms of everyone's whereabouts soon thereafter. Sure enough, McCarver raced home ahead of right fielder Oliva's throw — the peg was off-line, anyway — and the N.L. walked away with a 2-1 victory.

"I was on my own whether to bunt or hit away," said Wills, who obviously made the right decision.

McCarver, who at 24 was making his All-Star debut, was surprised that he became a key figure in the game — or was involved at all. "I didn't think I'd get in the game because Tom Haller (Giants) was still on the bench and he was voted Number 2 (in the balloting by managers, coaches and players)," McCarver said.

Alston said there was no real reason for playing McCarver and not Haller, although he acknowledged that "San Francisco was well-represented anyway." As for letting the lefthanded-

hitting Cardinal face Richert when Atlanta's righthanded-hitting Felipe Alou was available to pinch-hit, Alston said he wasn't playing a hunch. "He (McCarver) hits lefthanders pretty well," the N.L. skipper explained.

Although Wills said the heat made the game feel as though it lasted a week, the players had gone about their work quickly — the contest took 2 hours, 19 minutes — but expertly. As one Eastern columnist reported at the time, "The game was beautifully played, baseball at its best.... It was a super spectacle, artfully performed under the most oppressive conditions imaginable."

Great baseball it may have been, but the searing heat of that afternoon 43 years ago seemed to leave the only truly lasting impression of St. Louis' fourth All-Star Game. It is, after all, Casey Stengel's quote — not the splendid game itself — that lives on.

Joe Hoppel is a free-lance writer based in St. Louis.

Busch Memorial Stadium

N.L. 2, A.L. 1

American League	AB	R	H	RBI	BB	SO
Dick McAuliffe (Tigers) SS	3	0	0	0	0	1
Mel Stottlemyre (Yankees) P	0	0	0	0	0	0
h-Rocky Colavito (Indians) PH	1	0	0	0	0	0
Sonny Siebert (Indians) P	0	0	0	0	0	0
Pete Richert (Senators) P	0	0	0	0	0	0
Al Kaline (Tigers) CF	4	0	1	0	0	0
Tommie Agee (White Sox) CF	0	0	0	0	0	0
Frank Robinson (Orioles) LF	4	0	0	0	0	1
Tony Oliva (Twins) RF	4	0	0	0	0	0
Brooks Robinson (Orioles) 3B	4	1	3	0	0	0
George Scott (Red Sox) 1B	2	0	0	0	0	0
e-Norm Cash (Tigers) PH-1B	2	0	0	0	0	0
Bill Freehan (Tigers) C	2	0	1	0	0	0
Earl Battey (Twins) C	1	0	0	0	1	1
Bobby Knoop (Angels) 2B	2	0	0	0	0	0
g-Bobby Richardson (Yankees) PH-2B	2	0	0	0	0	0
Denny McLain (Tigers) P	1	0	0	0	0	1
Jim Kaat (Twins) P	0	0	0	0	0	0
c-Harmon Killebrew (Twins) PH	1	0	1	0	0	0
d-Jim Fregosi (Angels) PR-SS	2	0	0	0	0	1
Totals	35	1	6	0	1	

National League	AB	R	H	RBI	BB	SO
Willie Mays (Giants) CF	4	1	1	0	0	1
Roberto Clemente (Pirates) RF	4	0	2	0	0	0
Hank Aaron (Braves) LF	4	0	0	0	0	1
Willie McCovey (Giants) 1B	3	0	0	0	1	0
Ron Santo (Cubs) 3B	4	0	1	1	0	0
Joe Torre (Braves) C	3	0	0	0	0	1
Tim McCarver (Cardinals) C	1	1	1	0	0	0
Jim Lefebvre (Dodgers) 2B	2	0	0	0	0	0
Ron Hunt (Mets) 2B	1	0	0	0	0	0
Leo Cardenas (Reds) SS	2	0	0	0	0	0
f-Willie Stargell (Pirates) PH	1	0	0	0	0	0
Maury Wills (Dodgers) SS	1	0	1	1	0	0
Sandy Koufax (Dodgers) P	0	0	0	0	0	0
a-Curt Flood (Cardinals) PH	1	0	0	0	0	0
Jim Bunning (Phillies) P	0	0	0	0	0	0
b-Richie Allen (Phillies) PH	1	0	0	0	0	1
Juan Marichal (Giants) P	0	0	0	0	0	0
i-Jim Ray Hart (Giants) PH	1	0	0	0	0	1
Gaylord Perry (Giants) P	0	0	0	0	0	0
Totals	33	2	6	2	1	5

American League	0	1	0	0	0	0	0	0	0	0	–	1	6	0
National League	0	0	0	1	0	0	0	0	0	1	–	2	6	0

American League	IP	H	R	ER	BB	SO	HR	BF
Denny McLain (Tigers)	3	0	0	0	0	3	0	9
Jim Kaat (Twins)	2	3	1	1	0	1	0	9
Mel Stottlemyre (Yankees)	2	1	0	0	1	0	0	8
Sonny Siebert (Indians)	2	0	0	0	1	0	0	6
Pete Richert (Senators) L	0.1	2	1	1	0	0	0	3
Totals	9.1	6	2	2	1	5	0	35

National League	IP	H	R	ER	BB	SO	HR	BF
Sandy Koufax (Dodgers)	3	1	1	1	0	1	0	10
Jim Bunning (Phillies)	2	1	0	0	0	2	0	7
Juan Marichal (Giants)	3	3	0	0	0	2	0	11
Gaylord Perry (Giants) W	2	1	0	0	1	1	0	8
Totals	10	6	1	1	1	6	0	36

a-Grounded out for Koufax in third. b-Struck out for Bunning in fifth. c-Singled for Kaat in sixth. d-Ran for Killebrew in sixth. e-Grounded into double play for Scott in seventh. f-Fouled out for Cardenas in seventh. g-Grounded out for Knoop in eighth. h-Flied out for Stottlemyre in eighth. i-Struck out for Marichal in eighth. DP: NL, McCovey-Cardenas-McCovey. LOB: AL 5, NL 5. 2B: Clemente. 3B: B. Robinson. SH: Hunt. WP: Koufax, Perry. Umpires: Changed positions in sixth inning to: HP - Jim Honochick, 1B - Ed Vargo, 2B - Frank Umont, 3B - Al Barlick, LF - Jerry Neudecker, RF - Bob Engel. Time: 2:19. Attendance: 49,936.

As real estate sat ready for redevelopment, the All-Star Game capped a Bicentennial Celebration for the Gateway City.

Office of the Mayor / City of Saint Louis, Missouri

ALFONSO J. CERVANTES, *Mayor*

WELCOME TO SAINT LOUIS:

       The City of Saint Louis is indeed proud to be the host to the major league All-Star game for the fourth time.

       This occasion is especially significant, because the game marks the final attraction in the celebration of our city's Bicentennial, and because it is being played in our new downtown Civic Center Busch Memorial Stadium, which is emblematic, along with the magnificent Gateway Arch, of the progress which our city is making.

       We welcome all the great players and officials of baseball, as well as all the fans of our national pastime. We hope you enjoy our city and its many attractions as much as you enjoy the All-Star game.

       Best wishes and

                                Kind regards,

                                Mayor

Feeling the heat

While the Cardinals grabbed headlines early in the first half of the 1966 season (see page 108), the city of St. Louis was making news, too – for the best and worst of reasons. It was busting its buttons over a spectacular national tourist attraction (the Gateway Arch, whose keystone had been inserted the previous October) and taking pride in downtown redevelopment (the jewel of which was lustrous Busch Memorial Stadium). But the upbeat mood took a terrible hit when a deadly heat wave consumed the St. Louis area just before the All-Star Game – and all its attendant hype – descended upon the city.

The oppressive heat that beat down on the city before, during and after the All-Star Game was reflected in local newspaper headlines that at first seemed typical for a St. Louis summer, then turned somber: "Mercury Hits 104, Pools Crowded," "50,000 in 103-Degree Heat See Humphrey Toss Out Ball," "All-Star Fans

Happy to Survive – Stadium Like Disaster Area," "28 Dead in Heat Wave, No Relief Is Sighted," "Heat Wave Death Toll Rises to 87," "City Suffers Its Fifth Consecutive Day of 100-Degree Readings."

When St. Louis fans opened their morning newspapers on game day, Tuesday, July 12, the front-page headline told of a blast-furnace temperature reading of 106 that had been reached the day before,

The big gala brought greetings from big names on the local and state levels, courtesy of official letters printed in the All-Star Game program.

Executive Office
Jefferson City
Missouri
65101

Warren E. Hearnes
Governor

July 12, 1966

TO ALL BASEBALL FANS:

May I take this opportunity to extend to all of you a most hearty welcome to Missouri and St. Louis.

Today is a day of which we are extremely proud because we play host to the annual All-Star game and the exciting performers who have been chosen by their fellow players to participate in this great classic.

We have had numerous thrilling moments with our Cardinals in St. Louis this year, but an All-Star game has to rank as a highlight of any season. It is fitting, too, that this honor should come to St. Louis, which is just winding up its Bicentennial celebration.

And, of course, it gives all of us from Missouri a great deal of pleasure to welcome you to our new Busch Memorial Stadium. Our state has always ranked as one of the finest baseball areas in the country, and we feel that we now have a ballpark that is just as remarkable as our fine fans.

We say welcome to the stars of the National and American Leagues, and to the officials of the game of baseball who are visiting with us; welcome to our state, St. Louis and this beautiful stadium.

We sincerely hope that all of you, fans and players alike, will come back and see us often.

                    Sincerely yours,

                    Warren E. Hearnes
                    GOVERNOR

★ 1966 ALL-STAR GAME ★

Two days before the game, the Cardinals pulled Bob Gibson off the N.L. All-Star roster after trainer Bob Bauman examined the pitcher's ailing elbow.

Vice President Hubert H. Humphrey delivered the ceremonial first pitch following a pregame caucus with All-Star managers Sam Mele (left) and Walter Alston.

and how Union Electric was appealing for help to avoid a blackout crisis. But the show would go on at Busch.

Two first-aid stations were readied at the stadium. Additional vendors were hired to meet the expected demand – and need – for liquid refreshments. Staying hydrated would be critical. Fans also took pains to dress appropriately to deal with what figured to be brutal conditions.

NBC shipped tons of air-conditioning equipment to St. Louis to make certain its mobile units remained cool so its national telecast would remain on the air.

As dreadful as the weather was, Busch was really more of a gigantic discomfort zone than a full-blown disaster area. The main first-aid room, located on the third level and manned by two doctors and four nurses, provided ice bags, cold drinks and air conditioning for anyone who had fainted or become dizzy. Its five beds and two stretchers saw plenty of use, too. Yet the city's real problems with the devastating heat and humidity occurred away

from the ballpark and involved the elderly, the sick and residents of low-income areas who lacked fans or air conditioning.

Gemütlichkeit for Gussie

Although the heat became the overriding story, All-Star week in St. Louis also was a time for reflection. In an editorial entitled "St. Louis' Sportsman of the Year," *The Sporting News* praised Cardinals owner August A. Busch Jr. for his role in the construction of the new ballpark, bringing the All-Star Game to the city and making the downtown revitalization possible.

"The All-Star Game will be the final event of St. Louis' bicentennial celebration," the St. Louis-based publication said. "No individual can take sole credit for St. Louis' new stadium or for bringing the 1966

All-Star Game to the city. But no man contributed more to the success of these two ventures than August A. Busch Jr."

The Sporting News also noted that "when the Cardinals were up for sale in 1953, there was a strong possibility they would be sold to outsiders and moved to another city – until Busch blocked the threat. Through his efforts, the club was sold to Anheuser-Busch."

And the sports weekly pointed out that "the new stadium and nearby redevelopment projects have been built with private capital. They might not have been built at all had not Busch persuaded his company's board of directors that Anheuser-Busch should contribute the first $5 million of the necessary $20 million in equity funding. In St. Louis, you can't say benefactor better than Busch."

Downtown business boom

Among those benefiting from the All-Star Game's presence in St. Louis were downtown restaurants and bars. One union official said those bustling establishments were "pulling willing workers off the streets to go to work."

Parking space was at a premium for the All-Star Game, but good news was emerging on that front: The new parking garage east of the stadium would be open, and it would accommodate 1,000 cars.

Resident All-Stars

St. Louis came up empty in the vote of managers, coaches and players that determined the Nationals' starting position players, but center fielder Curt Flood and catcher Tim McCarver were named reserves and Bob Gibson was selected to the pitching staff.

Gibson, who was 11-9 with a 2.21 ERA at the break but had been tagged for 16 hits and nine earned runs over 11 innings in his last two starts, was withdrawn from the game in a decision that may have had everyone's blessing except Gibson's. Bothered by a sore elbow and fighting the effects of what trainer Bob Bauman called a tired arm, Gibson – ever the fierce competitor – never really asked out but acquiesced when Cardinals officials, in conjunction with baseball's top brass, concluded that skipping the game was the prudent thing to do.

St. Louis Globe-Democrat columnist Bob Burnes wrote that "while the Cardinals didn't say so, they obviously feared that Gibson would start the All-Star Game, would be carried away by the excitement and put an extra burden on a tired arm. They didn't want him to pitch."

Early-arriving All-Star fans could glimpse two Cardinals players and a Redbirds coach in secondary All-Star roles. Rookie lefthander Larry Jaster, who had pitched two shutouts against the defending World Series champion Dodgers in the first half of the season but also had been banished to the minors for six weeks, and coach Bob Milliken pitched batting practice for the Nationals. Reserve catcher Pat Corrales was behind the plate for B.P.

Johnny Keane, who had directed the Cardinals to the '64 World Series title, was an All-Star spectator. Keane was looking for work – he had been dismissed as Yankees manager in early May.

St. Louisan James Cavanaugh, who as a St. Louis Browns batboy had taken on the same duties for the A.L. team when the All-Star Game was played at Sportsman's Park in 1940, also was on hand.

Tickets ... anyone?

Some fans found themselves with extra tickets when friends or family members begged off because of the heat, but newspaper reports indicated that unloading the tickets – even giving them away – was not easy.

A ticket scalper's dream this All-Star Game was not. How hot was it? Two Kansas City men wore women's straw bonnets with braided ties to the game. "Better than nothing," one said of his $1.50 piece of protection.

Pregame color

The *Globe-Democrat* reported that "the playing field was duded up with red-white-and-blue baselines."

Among the big names taking part in the pregame pageantry: Cardinals vice president Stan Musial, accompanied by Miss Red Bird, introduced the players from both All-Star squads, and Jane Morgan, star of "Can-Can" at The Muny, sang the national anthem.

Vice President Hubert H. Humphrey threw out the first ball. After the game, the Veep cooled off by taking a dip in Gussie Busch's pool at Grant's Farm.

Local boys make good

Indians pitcher Sonny Siebert, a graduate of Bayless High School in St. Louis and a baseball and basketball standout at the University of Missouri, was a late addition to the A.L. squad. A replacement for injured Cleveland hurler Sam McDowell, Siebert purchased 30 tickets for family and friends – and then went out and delighted everyone, himself included, by pitching two perfect innings in relief.

Another local product, Ritenour High School's Ron Hunt, played a small but crucial role in the game. The Mets second baseman, who entered the game at the top of the sixth inning, sacrificed McCarver to second base in the 10th inning to set up Maury Wills' game-winning RBI single.

Hometown scorecard

McCarver, an All-Star despite finishing third in the voting for N.L. catcher, said that "just being here (the All-Star Game) rates with playing in the World Series," which the Memphis native had done in '64. McCarver didn't have any great personal expectations for the game – before the contest, Keane had cracked, "You're just here for the player representatives' meeting aren't you, Tim?" – but he wound up igniting the N.L.'s winning rally and scoring the game's decisive run. He replaced starting catcher Joe Torre in the eighth inning; McCarver's line for the day: 1-for-1 at the plate, and one putout.

Batting for the first time in All-Star play, Flood was limited to a pinch-hitting cameo in the third, in which he grounded out. He had pinch run in his first All-Star appearance, in 1964, when he scored on Johnny Callison's game-ending homer that capped a 7-4 N.L. victory.

– Joe Hoppel

Catch the replay from any seat in your house.

AT&T U-verse℠ TV with Total Home DVR.

AT&T is a proud sponsor of the St. Louis Cardinals.

AT&T U-verse. Advance your TV.

> Record up to 4 shows at once on a single DVR.

> Record the game on 1 DVR. Play on any TV in your home.

CALL TODAY OR VISIT AN AT&T STORE / 1-800-ATT-4YOU / ATT.COM/UVERSETV

Nine future Hall of Famers lined up for a league that was in the early throes of a reign of dominance.

Reversal of fortune

Remember that ol' American League swagger? It was first evident, oh, from about the time Babe Ruth launched a home run in the third inning of the first All-Star Game – a contest that National League starter Wild Bill Hallahan of the Cardinals remembered with awe because he and his N.L. teammates "were on the same field as Babe Ruth."

That Hallahan himself had surrendered the homer to the Bambino is incidental. What matters is that the National League had an inferiority complex from the outset of All-Star play in 1933 – and for good reason, considering that great Yankees and Athletics teams had dominated World Series play from 1927 through 1932 (with only the 1931 Cardinals interrupting their title run). Then the Americans drove home the point that the N.L. really was

inferior, building a 12-4 lead in the All-Star series through 1949. Swagger indeed.

But that was then, this is now (as in 1966): "You read what an edge the National League has. How their pitching is better, how their hitting is better. It's as if we're supposed to go out there and concede the game." Speaking was A.L. starting pitcher Denny McLain, who was assessing his team's chances in the '66 All-Star Game at Busch Memorial Stadium in St. Louis.

Yes, the All-Star worm had turned that much. The National League, which took the lead in the post-World War II signing of black and Latin American talent (including such headliners as Jackie Robinson, Roy Campanella, Willie Mays, Hank Aaron, Ernie Banks, Frank Robinson, Roberto Clemente and Juan Marichal), went on a 14-5-1 All-Star run beginning in 1950 and shot past the

---

Two decades after they squared off in St. Louis' previous All-Star gala, Willie Mays was still a Giant — but playing on the opposite coast — while Ted Williams stood two weeks away from induction into Cooperstown.

★ 1966 ALL-STAR GAME ★

American League catcher Earl Battey got a new perspective on perseverance from A.L. batboy Jay Mazzone.

Americans in the overall series standings for the first time in 1965.

Intent on adding to their 18-17-1 series edge, the Nationals' 1966 roster featured seven players with 20 or more home runs and a pitching staff with a collective 2.10 ERA.

Blurring lines of distinction

As had been the case beginning in 1958, managers, coaches and players from each league selected the eight position-player starters for their club. The All-Star managers – Walter Alston of the defending World Series champion Dodgers and Sam Mele of the 1965 A.L. pennant-winning Twins – chose the pitching staffs and reserve players.

However, Commissioner William D. Eckert announced a notable tweak in the voting procedure, decreeing that starting outfield berths no longer would be determined on a left-center-right basis. Eckert figured that selecting the three best outfielders regardless of sector would strengthen the squads.

Reigning single-season home run king Roger Maris, in the throes of a terrible season with the Yankees, wasn't buying Eckert's decision. "It's not fair.... A left fielder may never have another chance," said Maris, a right fielder, who wondered why infielders weren't somehow subject to the same treatment.

The change in the voting procedure for outfielders produced telling results. Baltimore's Frank Robinson, Minnesota's Tony Oliva and Detroit's Al Kaline, all primarily right fielders, finished 1-2-3 in the A.L. balloting. Under the old system, only one of them could have started; now, all three would be in the lineup. The A.L. outfield alignment wound up being Robinson in left, Kaline in center and Oliva in right.

The N.L. outfield vote landed two right fielders in the starting lineup – the Braves' Aaron and the Pirates' Clemente. Aaron moved to left, where he had played when he first came to the majors.

When the votes were tabulated, two Giants (Mays and first baseman Willie McCovey) and two Braves (Aaron and catcher Joe Torre) headed the N.L.'s starting lineup. The Tigers led the way among the A.L.'s starting position players with three picks (Kaline, catcher Bill Freehan and shortstop Dick McAuliffe), and Mele made it four Detroit starters overall when he chose McLain as his lead pitcher.

Including reserves and pitchers, the N.L.-leading Giants had the most players on either roster, with six. The Orioles, baseball's dominant team at the break with an eight-game lead in the A.L. race, settled for four representatives, including starters Frank Robinson and Brooks Robinson. Brooks, known for catching anything hit his way at third base, was hitting anything thrown his way, too. In a bit of a statistical stunner, he was leading the majors at the break with 70 RBIs.

Crew mates

Managers Hank Bauer of Baltimore and Birdie Tebbetts of Cleveland served as Mele's coaches. Herman Franks (Giants) and Harry Walker (Pirates) were Alston's skippers-turned-lieutenants.

Famed Red Sox hitter Ted Williams and Yankees managerial icon Casey Stengel, both two weeks away from being inducted into the Hall of Fame, were on hand as honorary coaches for the A.L. and N.L. squads, respectively. Stengel had concluded his managerial career the year before with the Mets.

Jay Mazzone, who had overcome the loss of both hands to serve as batboy for visiting teams in Baltimore, was selected to work in the same capacity for the American League All-Stars.

Notably absent

Pirates center fielder Matty Alou, the N.L. batting leader at the break (based on at least 210 at-bats) with a .338 average, was among those overlooked in the voting process and roster additions.

Another deserving candidate not invited to St. Louis: Orioles slugger Boog Powell, whose 67 RBIs ranked second in the A.L. In a 16-game stretch ending just before the break, Powell drove in 28 runs. Pittsburgh's Manny Mota and Baltimore's Russ Snyder, both with fewer than 210 at-bats but hitting .352 and .347, respectively, also were bypassed.

Not-so-mighty Yankees

The Yankees' Mickey Mantle, an also-ran in the voting and bothered by a chronic knee condition and ailing shoulder, was left off the team when Mele picked his reserves.

A veteran of 14 All-Star Games, Mantle was struggling when outfield starters were announced in late June, but he then made a

Bound for his third Cy Young Award in his final season, Sandy Koufax made his first All-Star start.

★ 1966 ALL-STAR GAME ★

strong case for a place on the A.L. roster by swatting 11 homers in his last 14 games leading up to the break. Early reports indicated the Yanks asked that Mantle be omitted so he could rest up over the break, but the Mick later said he had communicated his desire not to be included on the A.L. squad.

Not only was Mantle absent from the game, so was the Yankees' mystique. After long dominating major league baseball and contributing many standout players to A.L. teams that had routinely throttled the N.L. in All-Star Games, the Yanks had fallen on hard times. A pennant winner just two years earlier, New York was buried in ninth place and landed only two players on the A.L. roster: reserve second baseman Bobby Richardson and pitcher Mel Stottlemyre. In 1957, the last time the All-Star Game had been played in St. Louis, the Yankees had placed eight representatives.

A reliever's lament

Orioles relief ace Stu Miller, who had a 7-1 record and 1.68 ERA at the break, was disappointed that he wasn't picked. "I think the whole theory of picking pitchers for the All-Star Game is wrong," Miller said. "They pick all starting pitchers even though relief pitchers have become such an important part of the game."

Mele did choose all starters for his A.L. staff, but the Nationals' Alston included relievers Claude Raymond (Astros) and Billy McCool (Reds) among his eight original pitching choices. Alston then added a third bullpen man, the Dodgers' Phil Regan, when Cardinals starter Bob Gibson bowed out because of injury.

Tricky travel

Besides dealing with the suffocating heat that had set upon St. Louis, baseball's brass had to confront a mechanics strike against five major airlines that threatened to make traveling to St. Louis a bit tricky. Some All-Stars had two or three airline tickets because of the roundabout methods needed to reach the Mound City. As it turned out, only Baltimore's Frank Robinson and Andy Etchebarren and Detroit's McLain ran into trouble – and McLain's problems were weather-related. The two Orioles had to take a bus from Baltimore to New York to catch a flight and didn't arrive in St. Louis until 9 o'clock the night before the game. McLain's plane was delayed in Minneapolis because of the threat of a tornado.

A first for Koufax

Sandy Koufax, the 30-year-old Dodgers marvel who had won 26 games in 1965 and 25 in 1963, captured four consecutive N.L. ERA titles and been awarded two Cy Young trophies, was given his first All-Star start. "Sandy has never had the honor of starting one of these games," said Alston, "and I think he has pitched well enough to deserve it."

"Well enough," in this case, meant 15 victories and eight double-digit strikeout games in the first three months of the season.

Koufax astounded his N.L. teammates by applying a warm rubbing compound over his body before going out into the 100-degrees-and-rising heat. "He does it before every game," pointed out N.L. "host trainer" Bob Bauman of the Cardinals. "His body is so used to it, it doesn't affect him as much as you would think it would."

Hard knocks

Besides losing St. Louis' Gibson, the N.L. was without Houston's Joe Morgan, who had been voted the starting second baseman. Morgan, sidelined on June 25 because of a kneecap fracture, was replaced in the lineup by Los Angeles' Jim Lefebvre. It was the first All-Star selection for Morgan, who made the trip to St. Louis nonetheless.

Cubs third baseman Ron Santo, also selected to start for the N.L., suffered a cheekbone fracture on June 26 and seemed questionable at the time for All-Star duty. But he was back in Chicago's lineup on July 4 and ready to go in St. Louis.

On the A.L. side, Indians fireballer Sam McDowell withdrew because of arm trouble and was replaced by teammate Sonny Siebert, who had tossed a no-hitter against Washington a month earlier.

Team angst

For all its mounting troubles in the All-Star Game, the A.L. seemed to have a real chance in this one after McLain hurled dazzling ball over the first three innings. As the game wore on, though, and the Americans became increasingly ineffectual against the N.L.'s impressive array of pitchers, doubts must have crept in as the contest moved into extra innings.

"Boy, I'd like to beat these guys so bad I can taste it," McLain said while tuning in the 10th inning from the clubhouse. Moments later, Los Angeles' Maury Wills ended the game with a base hit, and McLain threw a towel to the floor.

It was not all jokes and backslaps in the other clubhouse. Franks, the San Francisco pilot, was upset that both of his Giants standouts, Marichal and Gaylord Perry, were among the four pitchers Alston had employed. "He had eight pitchers. They're all All-Stars," Franks barked. "There's no reason Alston had to use both of mine. That burned me up and I told him so."

Wills, who had lost out to Cincinnati's Leo Cardenas in the voting for starting N.L. shortstop, was highly satisfied with the outcome, even if he was still miffed over his failure to start. Reminded that he probably wouldn't have been in the game in the 10th if he had started – and thus not in a position to provide heroics – Wills shot back: "Yeah, but I might have scored a run earlier."

Post-break wrapup

Wills and the Dodgers, five games out of first place at the break, wound up storming to the N.L. pennant, but they were swept by Baltimore in the World Series. The Orioles' Frank Robinson won the Triple Crown, and the former Reds star became the first player to win the Most Valuable Player award in both leagues. Brooks Robinson, meanwhile, remained a key cog in Baltimore's drive to the championship, although he managed only 30 RBIs after the break.

As for Koufax, his first All-Star start proved to be his last. After finishing the season with 27 victories and another ERA title with a mark of 1.73 – and winning his third Cy Young Award – Koufax announced his retirement on Nov. 18, six weeks shy of his 31st birthday. Increasingly troubled by his arthritic elbow, Koufax said he feared permanent injury to his arm if he continued his career.

– *Joe Hoppel*

Cardinals™ banking
only at Bank of America

Get the **Cardinals**™ logo on your checks, check card, credit card and statements.

Visit bankofamerica.com/Cardinals or your neighborhood Bank of America for more information.

Official Bank of the St. Louis Cardinals™

★ THE SEASON ★
IN SHORT ★

In the twilight of its history, the old Sportsman's Park closed its gates for good after a Cardinals-Giants finale on May 8.

The Cardinals weren't worldbeaters when St. Louis played host to the All-Star Game for the fourth time in 1966 – their eighth World Series crown was a year away – but they were unabashed attention-getters. On their way to a 39-43 record at the break, the Redbirds had closed down a storied ballpark, made a blockbuster trade and moved into an eye-popping new home.

On May 8, the Cardinals and their fans said goodbye to old Sportsman's Park/Busch Stadium, where the team had played since July 1920. It wasn't the best of going-away parties – St. Louis absorbed a 10-5 pounding at the hands of the Giants, who finished off a three-game series sweep, and only 17,503 fans showed up to bid the place adieu. The last Cardinals run at Grand and Dodier came via a home run off the bat of Mike Shannon.

Later that day, the Redbirds, badly in need of offensive thump, dealt lefthander Ray Sadecki (a 20-game winner for St. Louis in 1964) to San Francisco for first baseman Orlando Cepeda, one of the game's premier sluggers. Cepeda had been sidelined for most of the preceding season because of a knee injury but had crushed 146 homers from 1961-64. He'd also belted a grand slam against the Cardinals the day before the deal.

If the exit from the old park was anything but an artistic success, the opening of the new stadium – tucked between Walnut and Spruce streets running north to south and Seventh Street and Broadway west to east – was a rousing affair. With a throng of 46,048 on hand May 12, the Cardinals christened Busch Memorial by tying the game against Atlanta on a two-out single in the ninth by Jerry Buchek and winning it in the 12th on Lou Brock's base hit. Shannon collected the first hit by a Redbird in the team's new digs, drove in the first run (tripling home Buchek) and banged out three hits overall in the 4-3 victory on a brisk Thursday evening.

At 10-14 after their debut game at new Busch, the

★ 1966 ALL-STAR GAME ★

First-night patrons at Busch's inaugural game got an All-Star sneak preview — uncomfortable temperatures (in the 40s at game's end) and extra innings.

Cardinals were still feeling their way in the young season – no great surprise considering that in the offseason the club had traded away three-fourths of its infield from the 1964 World Series championship team. Gone were hugely popular third baseman Ken Boyer (dealt to the Mets) and shortstop Dick Groat and first baseman Bill White (both of whom were sent to the Phillies). Taking over were Charley Smith at third, Buchek at shortstop and George Kernek at first. Smith had been obtained in the Boyer swap, Buchek previously had contributed as a steady reserve for the Cardinals and Kernek was up from the minors.

Dal Maxvill, who had seen backup service over four seasons for St. Louis, eventually eased into the lineup at short. Kernek stumbled at the plate and gave way to veteran Tito Francona shortly before

St. Louis swung the deal for Cepeda.

From the time he was acquired until the All-Star break, Cepeda batted .329 and cracked eight homers, despite being sidelined two weeks because of an eye injury. The Cards nonetheless muddled along, residing in sixth place at the time of the All-Star Game.

Down the stretch

Righthander Bob Gibson not only missed the summer classic, but also was idle until July 23, when he returned with a six-hit shutout against the Cubs. Gibson finished 21-12 for St. Louis, which ended the season at 83-79 and in sixth place.

Remarkably, rookie lefthander Larry Jaster, who had shut out the Dodgers twice before the break, whitewashed them three more times after the All-Star Game. His 1966 log vs. Los Angeles: five starts, five shutouts, 24 hits (all singles) allowed. Jaster posted a 6-5 mark against the rest of the league.

Cepeda hit nine homers and drove in 37 runs in the second half as he warmed up for his role in leading El Birdos to the World Series title the following year.

Although Cardinals fans in 1966 wouldn't have to wait long to celebrate another championship, they would have to wait more than four decades for another All-Star Game to come to town. That wait, thankfully, ends this summer. — *Joe Hoppel*

Acquired in a postgame trade following the last game at old Busch, slugging first baseman Orlando Cepeda set the tone for a total team turnaround by the Cardinals in 1967.

THE *Cardinals* CONSTELLATION

Star-gazing across the 79 celestial events that form the history of baseball's All-Star Game, you'll find 96 Cardinals picked to represent the National League since the inaugural gala in 1933. Within that Cardinal-red galaxy, many have glittered, others have shown dully, but collectively they've left an astronomical impression on an annual summer spectacle originally envisioned as a one-shot exhibition.

By Joe Schuster

★1933★
Game of the Century

AMERICAN LEAGUE 4, NATIONAL LEAGUE 2
COMISKEY PARK, CHICAGO

It was conceived as "The Game of the Century." And Cardinals owner Sam Breadon opposed it from the start.

When the 1933 World's Fair came to Chicago in the middle of the Great Depression, it was billed as the "Century of Progress Exposition." To help draw visitors to the fairgrounds, which sprawled across the city's south side, *Chicago Tribune* sports editor Arch Ward proposed a one-time exhibition game between the best players in each major league – "the greatest ... ever scheduled," he declared when he announced it. Profits would help support indigent former players, and to increase the public's interest, fans would vote for the teams.

For Ward's dream game to become a reality, he needed the approval of every major league club owner. The American League voted unanimously in favor of the event, scheduled for July 6 at Comiskey Park, but three N.L. owners initially rejected the idea. Two of those clubs, the Boston Braves and New York Giants, opposed it for logistical reasons – they had a doubleheader scheduled at New York on July 5, and doubted their players could reach Chicago before game time.

Breadon's objection was philosophical: He didn't like the precedent, fearing the game would become an annual event, Ward reported in a July column discussing negotiations. Breadon worried that a midseason contest between the two leagues would diminish interest in the pennant races, creating another drag on attendance, which had declined by 31 percent from 1930 to '32.

Frankly, Breadon was notoriously tight. While other owners

Cardinals third baseman Pepper Martin dug in as the first batter in All-Star Game history. He drove in the National League's first-ever run in the sixth inning of the inaugural game.

announced they were trimming payroll because of the Depression, he told the *Associated Press* that salaries would be "slashed, not trimmed" for Cardinals players. When other owners considered reducing ticket prices to accommodate fans' leaner wallets, Breadon saw no need to, reasoning people with limited means would spend their money on other things – he mentioned cigarettes specifically – and not on baseball tickets.

Breadon eventually dropped his opposition to the game. After Ward assured him it would be a one-time event, Breadon agreed not to stand in the way if every other club owner supported it. Once Ward got the Braves-Giants doubleheader rescheduled for September, the game was on.

Voting in 56 newspapers nationwide, a half-million fans cast ballots for the two teams, which – as Ward had promised – were formidable. The two 18-man squads boasted 20 future Hall of Famers, including Babe Ruth, Lou Gehrig, Jimmie Foxx, Al Simmons and Lefty Grove in the American League, and Pie Traynor, Paul Waner, Frankie Frisch, Bill Terry and Carl Hubbell for the Nationals.

The Cardinals, riding the success of five pennants and three World Series titles from 1926-34, placed four players in the N.L. starting lineup, tying the Yankees for the most All-Star starters: third baseman Pepper Martin, second baseman Frisch, catcher Jimmie Wilson and pitcher Bill Hallahan. All but Wilson stamped their presence on the gala.

True to the form that inspired his nickname, "Wild Bill," Hallahan walked five batters in two-plus innings – a single-game All-Star record for walks by one pitcher entering 2009. As the National League's first-ever starting pitcher, he was its first loser, as well. Before departing in the third inning with the N.L. in a 3-0 hole, he surrendered the first All-Star homer, a two-run clout by Ruth. Hallahan also notched the glitter game's first strikeout, catching the Babe looking in the first inning.

Martin had the honor of leading off the game, grounding out to shortstop. In the sixth inning, he drove in the Nationals' first run, scoring pitcher Lon Warneke from third on a groundout. One batter later, Frisch blasted the Nationals' first home run, off Washington's General Crowder. The Cardinals playing-manager added an eighth-inning single off Grove.

In due course, Breadon retreated from his initial opposition to the game. After his death in 1950, Ward wrote, "(Although) Breadon ... objected to (the) proposal for a midseason test between the stars of the two leagues ... he lived to become one of the game's staunchest supporters."

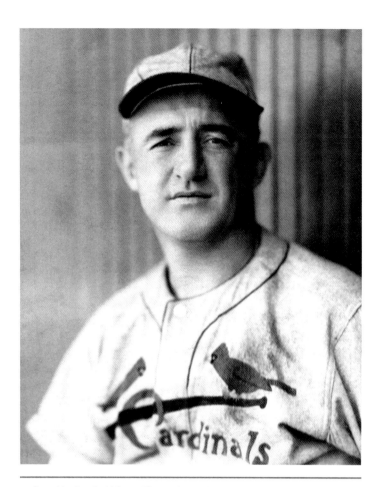

Switch-hitter Frankie Frisch blasted the National League's first All-Star home run, in the 1933 classic. He made more history with his second Dream Game homer, in 1934, becoming the first All-Star to go deep from each side of the plate.

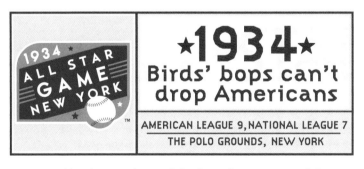

★1934★
Birds' bops can't drop Americans

AMERICAN LEAGUE 9, NATIONAL LEAGUE 7
THE POLO GROUNDS, NEW YORK

Inspired by the popularity of the first All-Star Game, club owners voted to have an encore in 1934. If it enjoyed similar success, they planned to make the exhibition an annual attraction.

With the "Gas House Gang" Cardinals making national headlines en route to a World Series title, four Redbirds headed for a sold-out Polo Grounds to join the National League's All-Stars. Frankie Frisch and Pepper Martin made their second straight appearance, joined by left fielder Joe Medwick and pitcher Dizzy Dean, a 14-game winner destined for a final record of 30-7 and a league MVP award. While Dean's star power and braggadocio reigned dominant throughout the season, on this day even he couldn't subdue a formidable American League squad all by himself.

The switch-hitting Frisch – who had homered from the left side in the inaugural All-Star Game – woke up an A.L. starting lineup of nine future Hall of Famers with a leadoff homer in the bottom of the first, batting righthanded. Two innings later, Medwick followed his manager's lead and blasted a three-run shot into the left-field upper deck. As the first pair of teammates to homer in the Midsummer Classic, they staked the N.L. to a 4-0 lead after three innings.

Dizzy Dean, the N.L. starter and winning pitcher in the 1936 All-Star Game, suffered a career-altering injury in the '37 gala, one batter after surrendering a home run to the Yankees' Lou Gehrig (left).

★1936★
Diz dusts off the A.L.

NATIONAL LEAGUE 4, AMERICAN LEAGUE 3
BRAVES FIELD, BOSTON

Helping the National League to its first All-Star victory, Dizzy Dean showed the Americans the kind of stuff that had produced 58 wins for the Cardinals over the previous two seasons. Awarded the start for the Nationals, Diz earned the "W" by pitching hitless ball over three innings, then reasoned he hadn't been up to par.

"You'd have seen something if I was feeling really good," he said. "I had all of my speed but I wasn't at my best."

Grousing that he'd struck out in his only at-bat, Dean took the opportunity to chide the American Leaguers. "I don't understand why I didn't get a hit. Anyone should be able to hit those American League pitchers. They throw nothing but 'nothing balls.' As for their sluggers ... they ought to get down on their knees and give thanks they don't have to work in our league, where they would see good pitching every day."

★1937★
Losing a toehold

AMERICAN LEAGUE 8, NATIONAL LEAGUE 3
GRIFFITH STADIUM, WASHINGTON, D.C.

Never mind the final score.

In our nation's capital and elsewhere, war was in the wind, the Depression wasn't easing up fast enough and it was blistering hot. That didn't stop Franklin D. Roosevelt from becoming the first president to attend an All-Star Game. On a scorching Wednesday afternoon, Roosevelt pulled his motorcade into Griffith Stadium, threw out the ceremonial first pitch and cheered for the American League as it handed the N.L. its fourth defeat in five All-Star meetings.

For St. Louis fans, there was an even bigger loss.

With two outs in the third inning, N.L. starter Dizzy Dean delivered what turned out to be the last pitch of his All-Star career. Future Hall of Famer Earl Averill lined it back up the middle, striking the pitcher's left foot. The ball caromed to Cubs second baseman Billy Herman, who threw out Averill to end the inning. Dean walked off the field, the victim of what initially was believed to be a bruised big toe.

The next day's papers didn't report the extent of Dean's toe problem. History did. Diz had, in fact, suffered a broken toe. And when he tried to return to the Cardinals rotation before the toe had healed, he altered his pitching motion and permanently damaged his famed right arm. He was never the same. By 1938, the pride of St. Louis was a Cub. Dean's record

By the time Dean took the mound to start the sixth inning, the Americans had erupted for eight runs. They'd get another off Dean in the sixth, but the Cardinals ace settled down to finish his three-inning stint without further damage and with four strikeouts to his credit.

While Dean helped restore sanity to a game that was getting out of hand, his performance was no better than second-best to the magic performed by one of his frequent regular-season adversaries, Giants lefthander Carl Hubbell. As the N.L. starter, the screwball specialist struck out, in succession, five future Hall of Fame legends: Babe Ruth, Lou Gehrig and Jimmie Foxx in the first inning, then Al Simmons and Joe Cronin to start the second. Hubbell finished with six strikeouts (he fanned Lefty Gomez to end the second inning) in three shutout frames.

On his way to winning the 1937 Triple Crown and N.L. MVP award, Joe Medwick established an All-Star record with four hits in the July 7 game in the nation's capital.

in five-plus seasons before the 1937 All-Star Game: 133-72. In the 4½ seasons after his fateful outing: 17-11, not even equal to a single season during his prime.

While the game was disastrous for Dean – besides the injury, he was handed the loss for surrendering a two-run homer to Lou Gehrig one batter before Averill – the Cardinals' Joe Medwick was the hitting star. On his way that season to an MVP award and a Triple Crown (the last recorded in the National League), he became the first player to collect four hits – two doubles and a pair of singles – in an All-Star Game (a record since matched by Ted Williams and Carl Yastrzemski).

★1948★
A blast for the home crowd

AMERICAN LEAGUE 5, NATIONAL LEAGUE 2
SPORTSMAN'S PARK, ST LOUIS

With the war and the Depression long gone, prosperity seemed to be everywhere but in the National League at All-Star time. In the first 14 Dream Games, the Nationals had lost a nightmarish 10 times.

As St. Louis welcomed the midsummer gala for a second time – this year the Browns were the host club – the Cardinals placed three future Hall of Famers in the N.L. starting lineup: Stan Musial (the league's leading vote getter) in left field, Red Schoendienst at second base and Enos Slaughter in right field. Redbirds lefty Harry Brecheen, headed for the only 20-victory season of his career, also suited up for the classic.

Three batters into the game, Musial gave the home crowd something to celebrate. With Richie Ashburn on third, Musial leaned into an 0-2 pitch and drove it more than 400 feet into right-center, onto Sportsman's Park's pavilion roof, for the first of what would be a record six career All-Star home runs.

Nonetheless, as *The New York Times* reported the next day, "That was the Nationals' opening and closing shot." The Americans gave the Browns a 1-0 all-time record as All-Star host, thanks to Yankees pitcher Vic Raschi. Contributing a two-run single that put the A.L. ahead to stay, Raschi pitched three scoreless innings to earn the victory – the last recorded by a Yankee in All-Star competition.

★1949★
The Man and the rookie

AMERICAN LEAGUE 11, NATIONAL LEAGUE 7
EBBETS FIELD, BROOKLYN

Brooklyn's Jackie Robinson and Cleveland's Larry Doby broke the color line in the National and American leagues, respectively, in 1947, but they'd wait two more years to take the field in an All-Star Game. With Brooklyn's Ebbets Field hosting its first classic, Robinson and Doby were joined by Dodgers Don Newcombe and Roy Campanella as the first black players to participate in All-Star action.

Seven Cardinals All-Stars headed to Brooklyn, including two in the starting lineup: Stan Musial in center field and rookie Eddie Kazak at third base. They were joined by pitchers Howie Pollet and Red Munger, shortstop Marty Marion, second baseman Red Schoendienst and outfielder Enos Slaughter.

As he had done the previous year, Musial launched a two-run homer in the first inning, this time scoring Robinson ahead of him. Kazak, a .302 hitter entering the game, was perfect at the plate, with two singles in two at-bats: one in the second that eventually led to an N.L. run, and an RBI-single in the third that gave the Nationals their only lead of the game.

But the relentless Americans scored 11 times on a rainy afternoon noteworthy because six umpires were used for the first time (one arbiter was added on each outfield foul line), until Al Barlick inexplicably left the field after completing 4½ innings behind home plate.

Kazak never fulfilled the promise of the first half of his rookie season. Back at Ebbets Field less than two weeks later, he broke his right ankle sliding into second with a double. Doctors initially misdiagnosed the injury as a sprain, and Kazak didn't undergo surgery until the offseason. The damage had been done, however, and Kazak was no longer able to effectively pivot on his ankle. He appeared in only 120 games over the next three seasons before his big-league career ended.

★1950★
Red's called shot

NATIONAL LEAGUE 4, AMERICAN LEAGUE 3
COMISKEY PARK, CHICAGO

Red Schoendienst came off the bench to steal the spotlight with late-game heroics in 1950, leading the Nationals to a 4-3 victory with the first extra-innings homer in All-Star history.

There are days when a player *knows* he's going deep. Even a player who hit just 84 home runs over 19 major league seasons.

In the first Midsummer Classic to require extra innings, and the first one nationally televised, three Cardinals filled out the N.L. starting lineup as the All-Star Game made its first return to Comiskey Park, site of the inaugural 1933 gala: shortstop Marty Marion, first baseman Stan Musial and center fielder Enos Slaughter. On the bench, Cardinal Red Schoendienst sat ready to relieve starting second baseman Jackie Robinson.

Slaughter helped the Nationals to a 2-0 lead in the second inning, tripling home Robinson and then scoring on a sacrifice fly. The N.L. wouldn't score again until the ninth, when Pittsburgh's Ralph Kiner tied the game with a solo homer.

The score stayed knotted until the 14th inning, when Schoendienst finally got his first turn at bat after taking over for Robinson in the 11th. Reporting later in the *Post-Dispatch,* Bob Broeg revealed that Schoendienst's 10-inning stint on the bench had prompted him to remark to two former Redbirds, Walker Cooper of the Braves and Murry Dickson of the Pirates (present as a batting-practice pitcher): "I wish they'd give me a chance. I'd put one up there," and waved toward the left-field stands.

And so he did. After disputing a borderline outside pitch called a strike, which put him in a 1-2 hole, Schoendienst drove the next delivery into Comiskey's left-field upper deck. Fittingly, he ended the game by turning the pivot on a 5-4-3 double-play grounder, retiring Joe DiMaggio in the Yankee legend's last career All-Star at-bat.

★1951★
Motor City mash-fest

NATIONAL LEAGUE 8, AMERICAN LEAGUE 3
BRIGGS STADIUM, DETROIT

On a day when the greatest hitter of the "dead-ball" era tossed out the first pitch, a record number of home runs flew out of Detroit's Briggs Stadium as the National League won back-to-back All-Star Games for the first time.

After Ty Cobb's ceremonial first pitch, the game stood just 1-1 after three innings. A.L. starting pitcher Ned Garver, the only Browns hurler ever to start an All-Star Game, contributed a respectable three frames, allowing just one hit and an unearned run. An 11-4 pitcher at the break, Garver had recorded half of the last-place Browns' 22 victories.

Things came alive at the start of the fourth inning, when Stan Musial slammed the first pitch from Yankee Eddie Lopat for a home run. The drive gave the N.L. a lead it never surrendered, with three more National Leaguers – Ralph Kiner, Bob Elliott and Gil Hodges – connecting for home runs. Including A.L. home runs from George Kell and Vic Wertz, the six-homer gala established a single-game All-Star record

(including an RBI-single off Paige), scored two runs and finished his All-Star career with a .381 average (8-for-21) – second among Cardinals (with at least 10 All-Star at-bats) to Albert Pujols' .429 mark (6-for-14).

★1954★
Red-faced

AMERICAN LEAGUE 11, NATIONAL LEAGUE 9
MUNICIPAL STADIUM, CLEVELAND

National League All-Star fixtures Ralph Kiner and Stan Musial combined for six home runs in the four Dream Games played between 1948 and 1951.

Although he led the National League with 26 steals as a rookie in 1945, Red Schoendienst didn't make it to the Hall of Fame as a base thief. He concluded his career with just 89 stolen bases in more than 2,200 games.

But in a wild All-Star slugfest witnessed by 69,751 fans at Cleveland's cavernous Municipal Stadium, Schoendienst's unsuccessful attempt to steal home in the eighth inning may have tilted the game toward the American League.

When Schoendienst batted in the top of the inning with two outs, the National League had just taken a 9-8 lead on a two-run pinch-homer by Cincinnati's Gus Bell – the fifth home run of the day. Reaching on a two-base error when Minnie Minoso

matched three years later at Cleveland, and exactly two decades later ... back in Detroit.

★1953★
Swan songs

NATIONAL LEAGUE 5, AMERICAN LEAGUE 1
CROSLEY FIELD, CINCINNATI

In 1953, playing his final season as a Cardinal, Enos Slaughter embellished a glowing All-Star resume topped by a .381 career average in 10 games.

Neither Enos Slaughter nor the Browns knew it at the All-Star break, but 1953 would be their last season in St. Louis. The Brownies moved to Baltimore and became the Orioles in 1954, while "Country" cried and departed for New York to become a Yankee, traded two days before the season opener.

The last Browns players to appear in the Midsummer Classic were a generation apart. Shortstop Billy Hunter, a 25-year-old rookie, made his only career All-Star appearance, pinch-running for Mickey Mantle. Former Negro leagues legend Satchel Paige, believed to be 47, pitched the eighth in relief, allowing the Nationals' final two runs.

Slaughter, 37, made the last of his 10 All-Star appearances – fourth all-time among Cardinals. He made a sensational diving catch of a line drive by Harvey Kuenn, rapped two hits

After 4⅓ innings of scoreless relief from Gene Conley (left) and Joe Nuxhall,
Stan Musial led off the 12th inning of the 1955 gala with a walk-off homer,
capping a six-run National League comeback win.

dropped his fly ball to right, Schoendienst advanced to third on a single, bringing up the N.L.'s leading hitter, Brooklyn's Duke Snider at .363.

With the count 1-1, third-base coach Leo Durocher made the call to send Schoendienst home, reasoning the sight of a runner barreling down the line would rattle A.L. rookie pitcher Dean Stone of Washington, causing him to commit a crucial run-producing balk. But Stone's delivery to Yankees catcher Yogi Berra arrived well ahead of Schoendienst, who was called out by plate umpire Bill Stewart.

Durocher, joined by first-base coach Charlie Grimm, threw a fit, claiming Stone failed to come to a stop in his motion before he threw. "That call was a disgrace," Durocher roared afterward. "Every person in the ballpark saw the play except the one man who should have. He ... cost us one run for sure and no telling how many more."

The A.L. scored three times in the bottom of the inning, helped by a home run from the Indians' Larry Doby, to reclaim the lead and halt the Nationals' winning streak at four games.

Stone, who entered the game to pitch to Snider, received credit for the victory without retiring a batter.

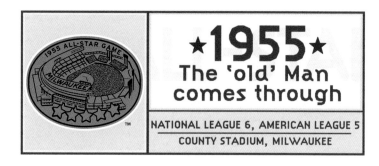

★1955★
The 'old' Man
comes through

NATIONAL LEAGUE 6, AMERICAN LEAGUE 5
COUNTY STADIUM, MILWAUKEE

When Stan Musial strode to the plate to lead off the bottom of the 12th inning in the 1955 All-Star Game, he hadn't distinguished himself for the usual noble reasons.

Voted a starter by fans in the previous seven All-Star events, Musial had been generally ineffective in this game, which he attended as a reserve selected by N.L. manager Leo Durocher.

After entering in the fourth inning as a pinch hitter, Musial had struck out, hit into a double play, grounded out and walked.

By his own admission, Musial was feeling old that year. Then 34 and in his 14th major league season, he had said as much when *St. Louis Globe-Democrat* sports editor Bob Burnes asked what he thought about establishing a record that year with selection to his 12th All-Star Game.

"It gives the other guys a perfect right to put the word 'old' in front of whatever else they're calling you," said Musial. "And now you start to feel they mean it.... You can't argue about the 'old' part of it."

As the self-confessed old man stood in the batter's box against the Red Sox's Frank Sullivan, he turned to catcher Yogi Berra and sighed, "You know, Yogi, I'm getting pretty tired."

"Me, too," admitted Berra, who had caught the entire game.

"Well," Musial reportedly said as he stepped into the first pitch, driving it deep over the right-field fence.

As Musial circled the bases, his National League teammates raced onto the field, greeting him at home as he leapt jubilantly onto the plate. The game-ending blast, just the second walk-off homer in All-Star history, was a record blow for Musial – his fourth in All-Star play, breaking a tie with Pittsburgh's Ralph Kiner and Boston's Ted Williams.

★1956★
Saluting 'The Captain'

NATIONAL LEAGUE 7, AMERICAN LEAGUE 3
GRIFFITH STADIUM, WASHINGTON, D.C.

When great third basemen are talked about, Ken Boyer deserves a long discussion. He won five Gold Gloves and an MVP award, was selected to 11 N.L. All-Star squads and anchored a World Series champion. He was a natural leader. To his Cardinals teammates, he'll always be "The Captain."

Boyer's remarkable performance in the 1956 All-Star Game remains a tribute to his greatness – unfortunately, it happened three decades before ESPN made highlight clips ubiquitous.

Making his first All-Star appearance, Boyer went 3-for-5 with an RBI and staged a defensive clinic with three dazzling plays. In the first inning, leadoff batter Harvey Kuenn smashed a line drive that appeared headed for the left-field alley, but Boyer made a diving catch. In the fifth, Kuenn again lashed a hard liner. Boyer dove to his backhand, snagged it on a bounce, scrambled to his feet and threw to first for the out, the crowd roaring its appreciation. In the seventh, he robbed Ray Boone of a hit with a leaping catch. Reporting in *The New York Times*, Arthur Daley mused: "If Harvey Kuenn has Ken Boyer hauled into Federal Court here on charges of grand larceny, no judge could withhold any sentence except guilty."

Boyer's performance eclipsed even Musial's on that day in the

Third in franchise history with 11 All-Star selections, Ken Boyer made a dazzling Dream Game debut in 1956, going 3-for-5 while playing highlight-reel defense.

nation's capital. Days after being named "Player of the Decade" by *The Sporting News* for the years following World War II, Musial extended his All-Star home run record when he connected for his fifth career blast. The seventh-inning solo shot landed deep in the left-center field bleachers in what was the last Midsummer Classic played at Griffith Stadium.

★1960★
No. 6 hits No. 6

NATIONAL LEAGUE 6, AMERICAN LEAGUE 0
YANKEE STADIUM, NEW YORK

From 1959 through 1962, two All-Star Games were played each summer, principally to generate additional revenue for the players' pension fund and youth baseball, and to help former major leaguers who had played before the start of the fund.

The twice-annual games were generally played about three weeks apart, but the two 1960 galas were staged within two days of one another. After singling as a pinch-batter in Game No. 1, played at Kansas City with the temperature reaching 101 degrees, Musial connected for his final All-Star homer in Game No. 2, at New York.

With Yankee Stadium slightly more than half full and the N.L. leading, 3-0, Musial came to bat as a pinch hitter in the top of the seventh inning, facing former Cardinals teammate Jerry Staley, now with the White Sox, who was pitching in his only All-Star Game. Musial blasted what one effusive report described as a "majestic Musial cannonade" that went "soaring into the upper deck."

Convinced it was Musial's last All-Star Game – he'd turn 40 later that year and would, for the second time in his career, finish at under .300 – the New York crowd gave Musial a standing ovation as he circled the bases and trotted into the dugout. In the *Post-Dispatch*, Bob Broeg reported that Sid Keener, a former sports editor from St. Louis who had become director of the National Baseball Hall of Fame, arose and left the ballpark. Keener assumed it was Musial's All-Star swan song and declared, "I've seen him go out the way I want to remember him." Musial went on to appear in five more All-Star Games.

Cardinals teammate Ken Boyer, though ailing with a severely strained side muscle, blasted a two-run homer in the ninth inning, making the two Redbirds the fourth pair of teammates to homer in the same All-Star Game – after Cardinals Frankie Frisch and Joe Medwick became the first pair in 1934.

In an era when All-Star lineups were selected by a poll of players, coaches and managers, four Cardinals formed the starting infield for the 1963 National League team: (from left) Bill White, Julian Javier, Dick Groat and Ken Boyer.

★1961★
There Are Ties in Baseball

NATIONAL LEAGUE 1, AMERICAN LEAGUE 1
FENWAY PARK, BOSTON

There may be "no crying in baseball," but there are occasionally ties. For the first time in history, the All-Star Game ended in a deadlock when heavy rain prompted umpires to cancel further action after nine innings. The Cardinals' Bill White, the N.L. starter at first base, tied the game with a run-scoring single in the sixth. The future league president had two of the Nationals' five hits in the second gala of '61.

★1963★
A great wall of Cardinals, and a last hurrah

NATIONAL LEAGUE 5, AMERICAN LEAGUE 3
MUNICIPAL STADIUM, CLEVELAND

Watching the 1963 All-Star Game on TV, where the infield defense gets on camera a lot, viewers might have thought the National League only bothered to send Cardinals to Cleveland, based on the voting for starting lineups by players, coaches and managers. Of course, you couldn't go wrong with an infield of Ken Boyer at third, Dick Groat at short, Julian Javier at second and Bill White at first. (Javier joined the starting lineup after Pirates second baseman Bill Mazeroski withdrew because of injury.)

Those Cardinals infielders seemed to be everywhere as they helped the National League to a 5-3 victory in a game that featured 16 singles among 17 hits overall. Groat drove in a second-inning run. White singled, stole a base and scored in the eighth. In the seventh, Groat made a good play on a ground ball by New York's Bobby Richardson and flipped to Javier for one out, with the relay to White completing an inning-ending double play. In the ninth, with the tying run at the plate and one out, White fielded another Richardson grounder and, with Groat, turned a game-ending 3-6-3 double play. Boyer was the only Redbirds infielder not at his position at game's end, after Ron Santo took over at third in the middle of the sixth.

Yet that was only a fraction of the Cardinals' All-Star news. A day after the club gave his old roomie Red Schoendienst his release as a player (Red became a full-time coach), Stan Musial made the last of his 24 All-Star appearances. Pinch-hitting in the fifth inning, he lined out to right field against Detroit's Jim Bunning, then received what the *St. Louis Globe-Democrat* called a "tremendous ovation" when he peeled off from the basepath to

The franchise leader among pitchers with nine All-Star invitations, Bob Gibson struck out three batters in two innings to preserve a 6-5 National League victory in 1965.

make his way back to the dugout.

Musial's final career All-Star statistics are testament to his year-in, year-out excellence: a record 24 games played (a mark he shares with Willie Mays and Hank Aaron); a record six home runs; tied with Mays for the most extra-base hits (eight) and total bases (40); and the highest batting average (.317) among an elite group of 10 All-Stars with 40 or more at-bats. He also ranks second all-time in All-Star hits, runs and RBIs.

The following season – with Musial in the front office and Schoendienst coaching– the Cardinals infield would be a key reason the franchise won its seventh World Series title, and first in 18 years.

★1965★
Gibson's 'save'

NATIONAL LEAGUE 6, AMERICAN LEAGUE 5
METROPOLITAN STADIUM, MINNESOTA

A year after winning the World Series, the Cardinals crumbled. They plummeted to seventh place – where they resided at the All-Star break – and broke up their nucleus at season's end, trading away three-fourths of the 1963 "All-Star infield": Ken Boyer, Bill White and Dick Groat.

One of the few bright spots was future Hall of Famer Bob Gibson, who notched the first of five 20-victory seasons in his career. As the Cardinals' only All-Star, Gibson displayed his competitive fire on a national stage, pitching out of danger in the last two innings to "save" the Nationals' 6-5 victory. (The save wasn't recognized as an official statistic until 1969.)

After striking out Detroit slugger Willie Horton to start the eighth, Gibson escaped a two-out jam with runners on second and third by retiring Minnesota's Jimmie Hall on a fly to Willie Mays, who made a leaping catch after he had slipped and nearly fallen. In the ninth, after the Twins' Tony Oliva led off with a double, Gibson retired the side, striking out future Hall of Famer Harmon Killebrew and the Yankees' Joe Pepitone to end the game.

The victory gave the National League its first-ever lead in the overall All-Star standings, 18-17.

Gibson would pitch in six All-Star Games and be invited to nine overall – more than twice as many as any other Cardinals pitcher. He started once, in 1972, in his last All-Star appearance.

Three seasons before he departed St. Louis, Steve Carlton got the start and the victory under All-Star manager Red Schoendienst in 1969.

★1966★
St. Louis scorcher

NATIONAL LEAGUE 2, AMERICAN LEAGUE 1
BUSCH MEMORIAL STADIUM, ST. LOUIS

With the temperature soaring past 100 degrees, the bats for both leagues wilted under the blistering sun in the fourth All-Star Game played in St. Louis.

With the game a pitchers' duel throughout, the A.L. scored first on a triple and a Sandy Koufax wild pitch in the second inning. The N.L. tied it with three singles in the fourth. Thus began five straight innings of scoreless "action," with only one player reaching base in the seventh through ninth innings.

It took a Cardinal to rescue what was left of the home crowd from further sun-related suffering. Appearing in his first All-Star Game, catcher Tim McCarver led off the bottom of the 10th with a sharp single to right. He advanced to second on a sacrifice, and when the Dodgers' Maury Wills punched a single into right-

center, McCarver broke for home, even though the outfield was playing shallow due to Wills' lack of power.

"Tim's pretty fast, it was worth the chance," reasoned third-base coach Harry Walker, a former Cardinals All-Star, who waved McCarver home.

McCarver beat the throw with ease, and for the third time in All-Star history, a Cardinals player scored the winning run in an extra-inning game.

★1969★
Lefty gets the victory

NATIONAL LEAGUE 9, AMERICAN LEAGUE 3
RFK STADIUM, WASHINGTON, D.C.

More than three decades after Dizzy Dean became the first Cardinals pitcher to win an All-Star Game, lefthander Steve Carlton become the second, getting the start with Redbirds manager Red Schoendienst at the N.L. helm. The future Hall of Fame pitcher wasn't his sharpest – he surrendered two runs on solo homers by Washington's Frank Howard and Detroit's Bill Freehan – but benefited from an even more potent N.L. offense that scored eight runs in the first three innings. Carlton contributed an RBI-double in the third, then gave way to another Cardinals hurler, Bob Gibson, in the fourth inning. In September, Carlton would set a single-game major league record that stood for nearly 17 years, striking out 19 batters, in a 4-3 loss to the Mets.

Rick Wise marked a two-season stay in St. Louis with a 1973 All-Star start, and win – the last victory recorded by a Cardinals pitcher in Dream Game competition.

★1973★
'W' for Wise

NATIONAL LEAGUE 7, AMERICAN LEAGUE 1
ROYALS STADIUM, KANSAS CITY

Acquired from the Phillies in 1972 in a trade for Steve Carlton, Rick Wise followed his predecessor's All-Star lead by getting the start and victory for the National League – the last time a Cardinals pitcher earned an All-Star win. Wise allowed a run in two innings, before being lifted for a pinch hitter in the third, when the N.L. scored two to take a lead it wouldn't relinquish.

"It's hard to believe no Cardinal has won an All-Star Game since I did," Wise told *Cardinals Gameday Magazine* this year. "But a lot depends on when you pitch in the game. There's definitely some luck involved."

★1974★
Reg-gie!

NATIONAL LEAGUE 7, AMERICAN LEAGUE 2
THREE RIVERS STADIUM, PITTSBURGH

This July marks the 35th anniversary of the last homer hit by a Cardinal in the Midsummer Classic. The last man to do it experienced one of a hitter's worst nightmares right before the big blow.

Reggie Smith, acquired by the Cardinals from Boston in an offseason trade that included '73 All-Star Game winner Rick Wise, led off the seventh inning against Oakland ace Catfish Hunter. Swinging hard at an 0-1 pitch, Smith lost his grip on his bat, which flew into the stands and struck a woman seated behind the first-base dugout. He hurried to the perimeter of the field to check on the woman, who assured Smith she wasn't seriously hurt. "A couple of guys tried to get the bat back, but I let the fan keep it," Smith said this year in an interview with *Cardinals Gameday Magazine.*

With a new piece of lumber in hand, Smith crushed the next pitch into the second deck at Pittsburgh's Three Rivers Stadium. Smith stood at the plate and admired the mammoth drive – his first All-Star hit after he wore the collar in the 1969 and '72 games.

"When I got back to the dugout, my teammates got on me pretty good and asked why I did that," Smith remembered. "I told them, 'Seventy million people are watching this game on TV, and I wanted to see the ball I hit, too.'"

Fellow Cardinals outfielder Lou Brock, running his way to a single-season record of 118 stolen bases, entered the All-Star break with 60 steals. Pinch-hitting to lead off the fifth, he lined a single off Boston's Luis Tiant, stole second base, continued to third when the throw by Yankees catcher Thurman Munson sailed into center field and scored on a sacrifice fly, putting the N.L. ahead, 4-2.

The 1979 All-Star Game was considered something of a victory lap for outfielder Lou Brock, who had announced in April that he would retire at season's end. At the time, Brock held the majors' all-time stolen base record and was approaching 3,000 career hits (a milestone he'd reach in mid-August).

But a tantrum by 23-year-old teammate Garry Templeton temporarily stole some thunder from Brock's last hurrah. In a fit of pique because fans had selected Larry Bowa to start at shortstop instead of him, Templeton, chosen as a reserve, declared, "If I ain't startin', I ain't departin'" – and made good on his word, staying home from the game. Undeniably talented – he finished the 1979 season with 100 hits from each side of the plate, becoming the first of only two hitters to do so – Templeton's fits of immaturity were a major reason he was traded

Talented but tempestuous shortstop Garry Templeton skipped the 1979 All-Star Game when he wasn't voted a starter.

Five Cardinals combined for 12 home runs in the 44 All-Star Games played before Reggie Smith (above) went deep in 1974; in the 34 classics played since then, no other Redbirds have cleared the fence.

★1979★
Brock's farewell,
Templeton's tantrum

50TH ALL-STAR GAME SEATTLE '79

NATIONAL LEAGUE 7, AMERICAN LEAGUE 6
KINGDOME, SEATTLE

to San Diego two years later, in a deal that netted Ozzie Smith.

As for Brock, selected to six All-Star squads in his career, he made the most of a second-inning pinch-hit appearance. Batting for former teammate Steve Carlton, Brock punched a single into right field to advance Bob Boone to second; two batters later, the Phillies catcher made it home on a sacrifice fly to tie the game, 3-3.

After the game, Brock waxed nostalgic for reporters, who painted him as humbled by his experience in the classic: "I'm glad I was a part of it," Brock noted. "It's going to be a little hard to watch all of this on television next July."

★1981★
Better late than never

NATIONAL LEAGUE 5, AMERICAN LEAGUE 4
MUNICIPAL STADIUM, CLEVELAND

The 1981 players strike, which darkened major league parks for 59 days, turned the 52nd All-Star Game into a hurry-up affair. The gala already had been postponed twice when players and owners agreed to a new collective-bargaining agreement in early August. The game was shoehorned in on Aug. 9, the latest date ever, on the day before regular-season play resumed. An All-Star record crowd of 72,086 came out for the event.

The wait was worth it for Cardinals closer Bruce Sutter, who had been acquired from the Cubs the previous offseason. The only pure reliever on the N.L. squad, Sutter entered the game in the bottom of the ninth, his team clinging to a 5-4 lead. He set down the side in order to add another save to an All-Star resume that already included two victories and a save.

★1996★
Ozzie says goodbye

NATIONAL LEAGUE 6, AMERICAN LEAGUE 0
VETERANS STADIUM, PHILADELPHIA

When N.L. manager Bobby Cox named Ozzie Smith to his 1996 All-Star squad, some writers complained that inclusion of "The Wizard," not even the Cardinals' regular starting shortstop at that point, cost more deserving players a roster spot.

But Cox was firm: "He's been the greatest shortstop in baseball for a number of years. It was my feeling that he belongs on the All-Star team."

Smith entered the game at short in the sixth inning and made his only plate appearance in the bottom of the seventh, with the N.L. holding a comfortable 6-0 lead. "The rousing ovation began as soon as (he) started for the plate," *USA Today's* Tom Pedulla wrote. "(He) became as emotional as his fans. He took off his helmet to acknowledge the crowd's roar.... It hardly mattered that Smith

In an emotional send-off at the 1996 game in Philadelphia, "The Wizard" capped an All-Star career featuring 15 invitations.

bounced out to second.... As he trotted toward the dugout, the crowd cheered as if he had homered."

When the A.L. batted in the ninth, Smith started a 6-4-3 double play, ensuring he went out on top in his last Midsummer Classic. Selected to 15 All-Star teams – 14 as a Cardinal – Smith was voted a starter by fans 12 times, tied for most in history at the position with Cal Ripken Jr.

★2002★
No winner, no Cardinals

NATIONAL LEAGUE 7, AMERICAN LEAGUE 7
MILLER PARK, MILWAUKEE

It was one of the most controversial calls in baseball history: With the score knotted, 7-7, after 11 innings, commissioner Bud Selig halted proceedings at the 73rd Midsummer Classic, producing only the second tie in All-Star history – and the first for reasons unrelated to weather. "The decision was made because there were no (extra) players left, no pitchers left," Selig said. "This is not the ending I had hoped for. I was in a no-win situation."

After dutifully following the "everybody plays" doctrine of present-day All-Star Games, managers Bob Brenly (N.L.) and Joe Torre (A.L.) approached the commissioner after the top of the 11th inning, concerned about the potential risk of injury to players if the game dragged into the night. When it was announced a tie would be declared if the N.L. didn't score in the bottom of the inning, the sellout crowd booed lustily, taking up chants of "Let them play!" and "Refund!"

The night had its share of somber moments. Before the game, video tributes played on the scoreboard to honor Ted Williams and two Cardinals – pitcher Darryl Kile and broadcaster Jack Buck – all of whom had died within the last month. Kile's No. 57 jersey hung in the N.L. dugout. The only Cardinal named to the Nationals' roster, pitcher Matt Morris, was at the game but unable to play, citing his grief over Kile's death and an irritated shoulder.

In the wake of the tie, All-Star rosters were expanded by two players.

★2007★
Pujols sits,
critics annoyed

AMERICAN LEAGUE 5, NATIONAL LEAGUE 4
AT&T PARK, SAN FRANCISCO

Mired in a decade-long winless streak, the Nationals appeared a lock to make it 11 years when they opened the bottom of the ninth with two quick outs facing a 5-2 deficit.

Over the course of the next five batters, the National League had pulled within a run, loaded the bases and set the stage for an epic comeback. Best of all, N.L. manager Tony La Russa had a plum pinch-hitting weapon at his disposal: Albert Pujols, the Cardinals' lone All-Star and the last position player available for duty.

Instead, mindful of the aftereffects of the 2002 All-Star tie at Milwaukee, La Russa chose to let Philadelphia's Aaron Rowand bat, and his fly ball to right ended the game.

Criticism of the decision was immediate, despite La Russa's defense that using Pujols could have put the Nationals at risk of forfeiting if the game had continued and one of their players were injured. "We're required to be ready to play extra innings," La Russa said. "So where are you going to use Albert? You can't use him. You've got to protect him."

In retrospect, La Russa acknowledged he missed a golden opportunity to inject Hollywood drama into baseball's midseason classic.

"If I had a chance to do it again, just to see Albert come out of the dugout in that situation – ninth inning, bases loaded – it would have been electric," La Russa told *Cardinals Gameday Magazine* this year. "For dramatics, that would have been the right decision. Strategically, it was not; we might have faced a forfeit if we went to extra innings.

"But entertainment is key at the All-Star Game. As the manager, I missed a chance to have one of the Top 10 moments in All-Star history."

After the game, Pujols oozed disappointment. "If I wasn't expecting ... to play, I wouldn't have come," he said. The previous evening, he had competed in the Home Run Derby, making it to the semifinal round.

Within a few days, Pujols softened. "I just told (La Russa) I was concerned for him because of all the ripping he was getting from the media," he said. "I didn't really care that much for myself, but I knew everyone was criticizing him."

Joe Schuster is a free-lance writer based in St. Louis.

The extent of Albert Pujols' 2007 All-Star contributions came one day before the game, when he slugged his way to the semifinal round of the Home Run Derby.

FOR THE FINEST IN DINING AND ACCOMMODATIONS

Player	Selections	Games Played	Games Started	Player	Selections	Games Played	Games Started
Stan Musial	24	24	14	Vinegar Bend Mizell	2	0	0
Ozzie Smith	14	13	11	Matt Morris	2	1	0
Ken Boyer	11	10	6	Reggie Smith	2	2	0
Enos Slaughter	10	10	5	Jerry Staley	2	0	0
Bob Gibson	9	6	1	Bruce Sutter	2	1	0
Red Schoendienst	9	8	4	Garry Templeton	2	1	0
Bill White	8	6	3	Lon Warneke	2	0	0
Marty Marion	7	5	5	Dick Allen	1	1	1
Albert Pujols	7	6	5	Luis Arroyo	1	0	0
Lou Brock	6	5	2	Don Blasingame	1	1	0
Joe Medwick	6	6	6	Kent Bottenfield	1	1	0
Ted Simmons	6	3	1	Jimmy Brown	1	1	1
Dizzy Dean	4	4	2	Orlando Cepeda	1	1	1
Larry Jackson	4	3	0	Royce Clayton	1	1	0
Whitey Kurowski	4	3	1	Curt Davis	1	0	0
Pepper Martin	4	3	2	Leo Durocher	1	1	1
Willie McGee	4	4	0	Pedro Guerrero	1	1	1
Johnny Mize	4	4	3	Bill Hallahan	1	1	1
Terry Moore	4	4	2	Tom Henke	1	1	0
Scott Rolen	4	2	2	Tom Herr	1	1	1
Joe Torre	4	4	2	Jason Isringhausen	1	0	0
Steve Carlton	3	2	1	Ray Jablonski	1	1	1
Walker Cooper	3	3	3	Felix Jose	1	1	0
Jim Edmonds	3	3	3	Eddie Kazak	1	1	1
Curt Flood	3	3	1	Darryl Kile	1	1	0
Frankie Frisch	3	2	2	Ray Lankford	1	1	1
Harvey Haddix	3	1	0	Ryan Ludwick	1	1	0
Mark McGwire	3	2	2	Stu Martin	1	0	0
Red Munger	3	1	0	Bake McBride	1	0	0
Howie Pollet	3	1	0	Lynn McGlothen	1	1	0
Edgar Renteria	3	3	2	Wally Moon	1	1	0
Hal Smith	3	1	0	Tom Pagnozzi	1	1	0
Lee Smith	3	0	0	Tony Pena	1	1	0
Joaquin Andujar	2	0	0	Ken Reitz	1	1	1
Harry Brecheen	2	1	0	Rip Repulski	1	1	0
Chris Carpenter	2	1	1	Del Rice	1	0	0
Jack Clark	2	2	1	Lonnie Smith	1	1	0
Vince Coleman	2	2	1	Bob Tewksbury	1	1	0
Ripper Collins	2	2	1	Bill Walker	1	1	1
Mort Cooper	2	2	2	Harry Walker	1	1	1
Joe Cunningham	2	1	0	Wally Westlake	1	1	0
David Eckstein	2	2	1	Burgess Whitehead	1	1	0
Dick Groat	2	2	2	Woody Williams	1	1	0
George Hendrick	2	1	0	Jimmy Wilson	1	1	1
Keith Hernandez	2	2	0	Rick Wise	1	1	1
Julian Javier	2	2	1	Todd Worrell	1	1	0
Gregg Jefferies	2	2	1				
Max Lanier	2	0	0				
Tim McCarver	2	2	0				
Lindy McDaniel	2	1	0				

You couldn't go wrong with a Dream Game infield anchored by third baseman Ken Boyer (above), an 11-time All-Star, and shortstop Ozzie Smith, a 15-time pick (once as a Padre).

1933: Frankie Frisch, 2b*; Bill Hallahan, p*; Pepper Martin, 3b*; Jimmy Wilson, c*.

1934: Dizzy Dean, p; Frankie Frisch, 2b*; Pepper Martin, 3b; Joe Medwick, of*.

1935: Frankie Frisch, manager/2b; Rip Collins, 1b; Dizzy Dean, p; Pepper Martin, 3b*; Joe Medwick, of*; Bill Walker, p*; Burgess Whitehead, 2b.

1936: Rip Collins, 1b*; Dizzy Dean, p*; Leo Durocher, ss*; Stu Martin, 2b; Joe Medwick, of*.

1937: Dizzy Dean, p*; Pepper Martin, of; Joe Medwick, of*; Johnny Mize, 1b*; Frankie Frisch, coach.

1938: Joe Medwick, of*; Frankie Frisch, coach.

1939: Curt Davis, p; Joe Medwick, of*; Johnny Mize, 1b; Terry Moore, of; Lon Warneke, p.

1940: Johnny Mize, 1b*; Terry Moore, of*.

1941: Johnny Mize, 1b*; Terry Moore, of*; Enos Slaughter, of; Lon Warneke, p.

1942: Jimmy Brown, 2b*; Mort Cooper, p*; Walker Cooper, c*; Terry Moore, of; Enos Slaughter, of.

1943: Billy Southworth, manager; Mort Cooper, p*; Walker Cooper, c*; Whitey Kurowski, 3b; Max Lanier, p; Marty Marion, ss*; Stan Musial, of*; Howie Pollet, p; Harry Walker, of*; Mike Gonzalez, coach.

1944: Billy Southworth, manager; Walker Cooper, c*; Whitey Kurowski, 3b; Max Lanier, p; Marty Marion, ss*; Red Munger, p; Stan Musial, of*.

1945: No game.

1946: Whitey Kurowski, 3b*; Marty Marion, ss*; Stan Musial, of*; Howie Pollet, p; Red Schoendienst, 2b*; Enos Slaughter, of.

1947: Eddie Dyer, manager; Harry Brecheen, p; Whitey Kurowski, 3b; Marty Marion, ss*; Red Munger, p; Stan Musial, 1b; Enos Slaughter, of*.

1948: Harry Brecheen, p; Marty Marion, ss; Stan Musial, of*; Red Schoendienst, 2b*; Enos Slaughter, of*; Eddie Dyer, coach.

1949: Eddie Kazak (r), 3b*; Marty Marion, ss; Red Munger, p; Stan Musial, of*; Howie Pollet, p; Red Schoendienst, 2b; Enos Slaughter, of.

1950: Marty Marion, ss*; Stan Musial, 1b*; Red Schoendienst, 2b; Enos Slaughter, of*.

1951: Stan Musial, of*; Red Schoendienst, 2b; Enos Slaughter, of; Wally Westlake, of.

1952: Stan Musial, of*; Red Schoendienst, 2b; Enos Slaughter, of*; Jerry Staley, p; Eddie Stanky, coach.

1953: Harvey Haddix (r), p; Stan Musial, of*; Del Rice, c; Red Schoendienst, 2b*; Enos Slaughter, of* Jerry Staley, p.

1954: Harvey Haddix, p; Ray Jablonski, 3b*; Stan Musial, of*; Red Schoendienst, 2b.

1955: Luis Arroyo (r), p; Harvey Haddix, p; Stan Musial, 1b;

Red Schoendienst, 2b*.

1956: Ken Boyer, 3b*; Stan Musial, of*; Rip Repulski, of; Fred Hutchinson, coach.

1957: Larry Jackson, p; Wally Moon, of; Stan Musial, 1b*; Hal Smith, c.

1958: Don Blasingame, 2b; Larry Jackson, p; Stan Musial, 1b*.

1959: (1st Game) Ken Boyer, 3b; Joe Cunningham, of; Vinegar Bend Mizell, p; Stan Musial, 1b; Hal Smith, c; Bill White, of.

1959: (2nd Game) Ken Boyer, 3b*; Joe Cunningham, of; Vinegar Bend Mizell, p; Stan Musial, 1b*; Hal Smith, c.

1960: (Both Games) Ken Boyer, 3b; Larry Jackson, p; Lindy McDaniel, p; Stan Musial, of; Bill White, 1b; Solly Hemus, coach.

1961: (Both Games) Ken Boyer, 3b; Stan Musial, of; Bill White, 1b*.

1962: (Both Games) Ken Boyer, 3b*; Bob Gibson, p; Stan Musial, of; Johnny Keane, coach (G1).

1963: Ken Boyer, 3b*; Dick Groat, ss*; Julian Javier, 2b*; Stan Musial, of; Bill White, 1b*.

1964: Ken Boyer, 3b*; Curt Flood, of; Dick Groat, ss*; Bill White, 1b.

1965: Bob Gibson, p.

1966: Curt Flood, of; Bob Gibson, p; Tim McCarver, c.

1967: Lou Brock, of*; Orlando Cepeda, 1b*; Bob Gibson, p; Tim McCarver, c.

1968: Red Schoendienst, manager; Steve Carlton, p; Curt Flood, of*; Bob Gibson, p; Julian Javier, 2b.

1969: Red Schoendienst, manager; Steve Carlton, p*; Bob Gibson, p.

1970: Richie Allen, 1b*; Bob Gibson, p; Joe Torre, c.

1971: Lou Brock of.; Steve Carlton, p; Joe Torre, 3b*

1972: Lou Brock, of; Bob Gibson, p*; Ted Simmons, c; Joe Torre, 3b*; Red Schoendienst, coach.

1973: Ted Simmons, c; Joe Torre, 3b; Rick Wise, p*.

1974: Lou Brock, of; Lynn McGlothen, p; Ted Simmons, c; Reggie Smith, of; Red Schoendienst, coach.

1975: Lou Brock, of*; Reggie Smith, of; Stan Musial, honorary captain; Red Schoendienst, coach.

1976: Bake McBride, of.

1977: Ted Simmons, c; Garry Templeton, ss.

1978: Ted Simmons, c.*

1979: Lou Brock, of; Keith Hernandez, 1b; Ted Simmons, c; Garry Templeton, ss; Dave Ricketts, coach.

1980: George Hendrick, of; Keith Hernandez, 1b; Ken Reitz, 3b*.

1981: Bruce Sutter, p.

1982: Lonnie Smith, of; Ozzie Smith, ss; Gene Gieselmann, trainer.

1983: Whitey Herzog, manager; George Hendrick, of; Willie

McGee, of; Ozzie Smith, ss*; Chuck Hiller, coach; Dave Ricketts, coach.

1984: Joaquin Andujar, p; Ozzie Smith, ss*; Bruce Sutter, p.

1985: Joaquin Andujar, p; Jack Clark, 1b; Tom Herr, 2b*; Willie McGee, of; Ozzie Smith, ss*.

1986: Whitey Herzog, manager; Ozzie Smith, ss*; Mike Roarke, coach.

1987: Jack Clark, 1b*; Willie McGee, of; Ozzie Smith, ss*; Gene Gieselmann, trainer.

1988: Whitey Herzog, manager; Vince Coleman, of*; Willie McGee, of; Ozzie Smith, ss*; Todd Worrell, p; Rich Hacker, coach; Nick Leyva, coach; Johnny Lewis, coach.

1989: Vince Coleman, of; Pedro Guerrero, dh*; Tony Pena, c; Ozzie Smith, ss.*

1990: Ozzie Smith, ss.*

1991: Felix Jose, of; Lee Smith, p; Ozzie Smith, ss.*

1992: Tom Pagnozzi, c; Lee Smith, p; Ozzie Smith, ss*; Bob Tewksbury, p; Joe Torre, coach.

1993: Gregg Jefferies, 1b; Lee Smith, p; Bob Gibson, honorary captain. Gene Gieselmann, trainer.

1994: Gregg Jefferies, 1b*; Ozzie Smith, ss*.

1995: Tom Henke, p; Ozzie Smith, ss.

1996: Ozzie Smith, ss.

1997: Royce Clayton, ss; Ray Lankford, of*.

1998: Mark McGwire, 1b*.

1999: Kent Bottenfield, p; Mark McGwire, 1b*.

2000: Jim Edmonds, of*; Darryl Kile, p; Mark McGwire, 1b; Edgar Renteria, ss; Brad Henderson, trainer.

2001: Matt Morris, p; Albert Pujols, 3b*.

2002: Matt Morris, p; Ozzie Smith, honorary captain.

2003: Jim Edmonds, of*; Albert Pujols, of*; Edgar Renteria, ss*; Scott Rolen, 3b*; Woody Williams, p; Tony La Russa, coach.

2004: Albert Pujols, 1b*; Edgar Renteria, ss*; Scott Rolen, 3b*.

2005: Tony La Russa, manager; Chris Carpenter, p; David Eckstein, ss*; Jim Edmonds, cf*; Jason Isringhausen, p; Albert Pujols, 1b*; Scott Rolen, 3b; Dave Duncan, coach; Marty Mason, coach; Dave McKay, coach; Jose Oquendo, coach; Joe Pettini, coach; Barry Weinberg, trainer.

2006: Chris Carpenter, p; David Eckstein, ss; Albert Pujols, 1b*; Scott Rolen, 3b.

2007: Tony La Russa, manager; Albert Pujols, 1b; Dave Duncan, coach; Marty Mason, coach; Dave McKay, coach; Joe Pettini, coach

2008: Ryan Ludwick, of; Albert Pujols, 1b*.

Denotes starter   (r) Denotes rookie

GOOD LUCK FROM YOUR FRIENDS IN BUSINESS

Field Staff

TONY La RUSSA
Manager-10

DAVE McKAY
First-Base Coach-39
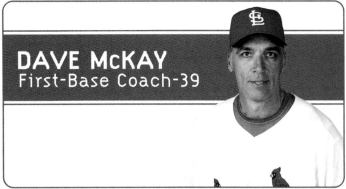

MIKE ALDRETE
Asst. Batting Coach-61

HAL McRAE
Batting Coach-15
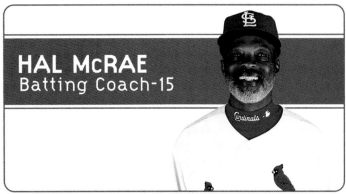

DAVE DUNCAN
Pitching Coach-18

JOSE OQUENDO
Third-Base Coach-11

MARTY MASON
Bullpen Coach-38

JOE PETTINI
Bench Coach-49

24

★ 20 09 ★

Ankiel

OUTFIELDER

HEIGHT: 6-FOOT-1
BATS: LEFT   THROWS: LEFT
BIRTHDATE: JULY 19, 1979
BIRTHPLACE: FORT PIERCE, FLA.

2008	AVG	G	AB	R	H	2B	3B	HR	RBI	SH	SF	HBP	BB	IBB	SO	SB	CS	GDP	SLG	OBA	E
ST. LOUIS	.264	120	413	65	109	21	2	25	71	0	3	5	42	3	100	2	1	8	.506	.337	8
MAJORS																					
6 YEARS	.262	222	672	105	176	30	4	38	119	4	7	5	61	3	170	3	1	12	.488	.325	17

★20 09★

Barden

INFIELDER

HEIGHT: 5-FOOT-11
BATS: RIGHT   THROWS: RIGHT
BIRTHDATE: APRIL 2, 1981
BIRTHPLACE: TEMPLETON, CALIF.

2008	AVG	G	AB	R	H	2B	3B	HR	RBI	SH	SF	HBP	BB	IBB	SO	SB	CS	GDP	SLG	OBA	E
ST. LOUIS	.222	9	9	0	2	0	0	0	1	1	0	0	0	0	4	0	0	0	.222	.222	1
MEMPHIS	.285	103	411	60	117	21	4	9	35	0	3	4	38	0	72	3	3	13	.421	.349	15
MAJORS																					
2 YEARS	.182	32	44	6	8	1	0	0	1	1	0	0	2	0	11	0	0	2	.205	.217	1

29

★ 20   09 ★

Carpenter

STARTING PITCHER

HEIGHT: 6-FOOT-6
BATS: RIGHT   THROWS: RIGHT
BIRTHDATE: APRIL 27, 1975
BIRTHPLACE: EXETER, N.H.

2008	W-L	ERA	G	GS	CG	SHO	GF	SV	IP	H	R	ER	HR	HBP	BB	IBB	SO	WP	BK	BAA
ST. LOUIS	0-1	1.76	4	3	0	0	0	0	15.1	16	5	3	0	0	4	0	7	0	0	.286
SPRINGFIELD	0-0	0.00	1	1	0	0	0	0	4	1	0	0	0	0	4	0	4	0	0	.077
MEMPHIS	0-1	3.18	1	1	0	0	0	0	5.2	4	2	2	0	2	1	0	5	0	0	.190
MAJORS																				
11 YEARS	100-70	4.08	250	232	25	12	6	0	1,537.1	1,576	768	697	174	57	468	13	1,171	44	2	.266

★ 20 ★ 09 ★

DeRosa

INFIELDER/OUTFIELDER

HEIGHT: 6-FOOT-1
BATS: RIGHT   THROWS: RIGHT
BIRTHDATE: FEB. 2, 1975
BIRTHPLACE: PASSAIC, N.J.

2008	AVG	G	AB	R	H	2B	3B	HR	RBI	SH	SF	HBP	BB	IBB	SO	SB	CS	GDP	SLG	OBA	E
CHICAGO (NL)	.285	149	505	103	144	30	3	21	87	2	8	9	69	0	106	6	0	9	.481	.376	1
MEMPHIS																					
MAJORS	.279	893	2,650	406	740	151	10	69	352	12	26	40	252	15	485	18	13	64	.422	.348	17
11 YEARS																					

16

UNCAN · CHRIS · DUNCAN ·

★ 20 ★ ★ 09 ★

Duncan

OUTFIELDER/FIRST BASEMAN

HEIGHT: 6-FOOT-5
BATS: LEFT   THROWS: RIGHT
BIRTHDATE: MAY 5, 1981
BIRTHPLACE: TUCSON, ARIZ.

2008	AVG	G	AB	R	H	2B	3B	HR	RBI	SH	SF	HBP	BB	IBB	SO	SB	CS	GDP	SLG	OBA	E
ST. LOUIS	.248	76	222	26	55	8	0	6	27	0	1	0	34	3	52	2	1	9	.365	.346	2
MEMPHIS	.160	7	25	5	4	2	0	0	3	0	0	1	4	0	5	0	0	1	.240	.300	0
MAJORS 4 YEARS	.266	302	887	139	236	40	3	50	143	0	4	3	119	6	249	4	2	18	.487	.353	10

31

★20 09★

Franklin

RELIEF PITCHER

HEIGHT: 6-FOOT-3
BATS: RIGHT   THROWS: RIGHT
BIRTHDATE: MARCH 5, 1973
BIRTHPLACE: FORT SMITH, ARK.

2008	W-L	ERA	G	GS	CG	SHO	GF	SV	IP	H	R	ER	HR	HBP	BB	IBB	SO	WP	BK	BAA
ST. LOUIS	6-6	3.55	74	0	0	0	39	17	78.2	86	34	31	10	3	30	4	51	3	0	.278
MAJORS																				
9 YEARS	51-67	4.19	390	106	6	3	92	18	1,047.1	1,080	523	488	155	46	312	28	565	13	6	.267

★20 09★

K. Greene

INFIELDER

HEIGHT: 5-FOOT-11
BATS: RIGHT   THROWS: RIGHT
BIRTHDATE: OCT. 21, 1979
BIRTHPLACE: BUTLER, PA.

2008	AVG	G	AB	R	H	2B	3B	HR	RBI	SH	SF	HBP	BB	IBB	SO	SB	CS	GDP	SLG	OBA	E
SAN DIEGO	.213	105	389	30	83	15	2	10	35	0	7	5	22	1	100	5	1	7	.339	.260	8
MAJORS																					
6 YEARS	.248	659	2,397	301	594	150	14	84	328	4	34	32	175	17	521	23	5	54	.427	.304	65

27

REENE • TYLER GREEN...NE • TYLER

★ 20   09 ★

T. Greene

INFIELDER
HEIGHT: 6-FOOT-2
BATS: RIGHT   THROWS: RIGHT
BIRTHDATE: AUG. 17, 1983
BIRTHPLACE: RALEIGH, N.C.

2008	AVG	G	AB	R	H	2B	3B	HR	RBI	SH	SF	HBP	BB	IBB	SO	SB	CS	GDP	SLG	OBA	E
SPRINGFIELD	.259	97	374	62	97	15	4	16	41	4	3	5	22	1	99	14	6	5	.449	.307	19
MEMPHIS	.234	30	111	17	26	7	0	0	7	2	0	4	11	0	35	6	0	1	.297	.325	4
MINORS 4 YEARS	.254	377	1,420	245	360	73	10	47	162	11	7	37	118	4	416	82	12	30	.418	.325	87

21
★20 09★
LaRue

CATCHER

HEIGHT: 5-FOOT-11
BATS: RIGHT   THROWS: RIGHT
BIRTHDATE: MARCH 19, 1974
BIRTHPLACE: HOUSTON, TEXAS

2008	AVG	G	AB	R	H	2B	3B	HR	RBI	SH	SF	HBP	BB	IBB	SO	SB	CS	GDP	SLG	OBA	E
ST. LOUIS	.213	61	164	17	35	8	1	4	21	3	2	5	15	1	20	0	0	6	.348	.296	2
MAJORS																					
10 YEARS	.231	842	2,559	294	592	144	7	92	337	20	18	102	229	39	731	13	11	68	.401	.317	48

26

★20   09★

Lohse

STARTING PITCHER

HEIGHT: 6-FOOT-2
BATS: RIGHT   THROWS: RIGHT
BIRTHDATE: OCT. 4, 1978
BIRTHPLACE: CHICO, CALIF.

2008	W-L	ERA	G	GS	CG	SHO	GF	SV	IP	H	R	ER	HR	HBP	BB	IBB	SO	WP	BK	BAA
ST. LOUIS	15-6	3.78	33	33	0	0	0	0	200	211	88	84	18	3	49	3	119	5	0	.272
MAJORS																				
8 YEARS	78-80	4.67	251	228	6	4	10	0	1,364	1,513	752	708	175	59	414	23	853	44	3	.282

47

★ 20 ★ ★ 09 ★

Ludwick

OUTFIELDER

HEIGHT: 6-FOOT-3
BATS: RIGHT   THROWS: LEFT
BIRTHDATE: JULY 13, 1978
BIRTHPLACE: SATELLITE BEACH, FLA.

2008	AVG	G	AB	R	H	2B	3B	HR	RBI	SH	SF	HBP	BB	IBB	SO	SB	CS	GDP	SLG	OBA	E
ST. LOUIS	.299	152	538	104	161	40	3	37	113	1	8	8	62	3	146	4	4	8	.591	.375	3
MAJORS																					
6 YEARS	.273	376	1,175	184	321	78	4	65	209	5	8	17	116	5	317	12	10	15	.512	.345	6

46

★20 09★

McClellan

RELIEF PITCHER

HEIGHT: 6-FOOT-2
BATS: RIGHT   THROWS: RIGHT
BIRTHDATE: JUNE 12, 1984
BIRTHPLACE: FLORISSANT, MO.

2008	W-L	ERA	G	GS	CG	SHO	GF	SV	IP	H	R	ER	HR	HBP	BB	IBB	SO	WP	BK	BAA
ST. LOUIS	2-7	4.04	68	0	0	0	7	1	75.2	79	37	34	7	4	26	2	59	6	0	.269
MAJORS																				
1 YEAR	2-7	4.04	68	0	0	0	7	1	75.2	79	37	34	7	4	26	2	59	6	0	.269

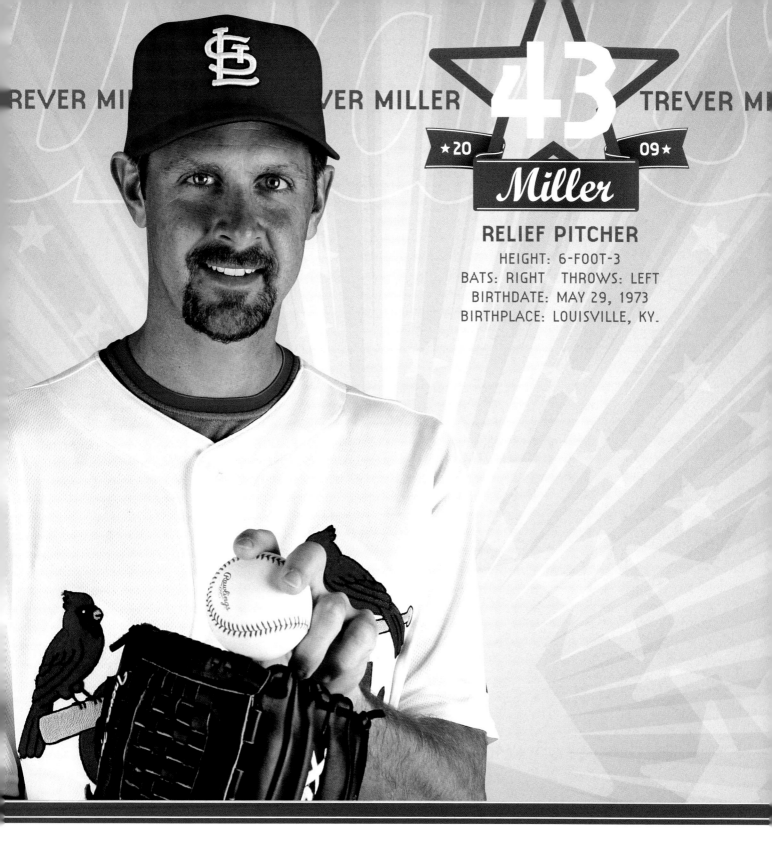

43

★ 20   09 ★

Miller

RELIEF PITCHER

HEIGHT: 6-FOOT-3
BATS: RIGHT   THROWS: LEFT
BIRTHDATE: MAY 29, 1973
BIRTHPLACE: LOUISVILLE, KY.

2008	W-L	ERA	G	GS	CG	SHO	GF	SV	IP	H	R	ER	HR	HBP	BB	IBB	SO	WP	BK	BAA
TAMPA BAY	2-0	4.15	68	0	0	0	16	2	43.1	39	21	20	2	4	20	1	44	1	0	.242
MAJORS																				
10 YEARS	14-14	4.43	519	5	0	0	116	10	422.1	435	227	208	45	37	198	25	354	15	0	.267

★ 20   09 ★

4

Molina

CATCHER

HEIGHT: 5-FOOT-11
BATS: RIGHT   THROWS: RIGHT
BIRTHDATE: JULY 13, 1982
BIRTHPLACE: BAYAMON, P.R.

2008	AVG	G	AB	R	H	2B	3B	HR	RBI	SH	SF	HBP	BB	IBB	SO	SB	CS	GDP	SLG	OBA	E
ST. LOUIS	.304	124	444	37	135	18	0	7	56	3	5	1	32	4	29	0	2	21	.392	.349	10
MAJORS																					
5 YEARS	.262	529	1,734	144	455	80	1	29	209	23	15	14	128	17	163	4	9	68	.360	.316	30

60

JASON MOTT

Motte
★ 20 09 ★

RELIEF PITCHER

HEIGHT: 6-FOOT
BATS: RIGHT   THROWS: RIGHT
BIRTHDATE: JUNE 22, 1982
BIRTHPLACE: PORT HURON, MICH.

2008	W-L	ERA	G	GS	CG	SHO	GF	SV	IP	H	R	ER	HR	HBP	BB	IBB	SO	WP	BK	BAA
MEMPHIS	4-3	3.24	63	0	0	0	28	9	66.2	64	25	24	6	1	26	3	110	7	0	.245
ST. LOUIS	0-0	0.82	12	0	0	0	4	1	11	5	2	1	0	0	3	0	16	0	0	.139
MAJORS																				
1 YEAR	0-0	0.82	12	0	0	0	4	1	11	5	2	1	0	0	3	0	16	0	0	.139

★20   09★

Pineiro

STARTING PITCHER

HEIGHT: 6-FOOT-1

BATS: RIGHT   THROWS: RIGHT

BIRTHDATE: SEPT. 25, 1978

BIRTHPLACE: RIO PIEDRAS, P.R.

2008	W-L	ERA	G	GS	CG	SHO	GF	SV	IP	H	R	ER	HR	HBP	BB	IBB	SO	WP	BK	BAA
ST. LOUIS	7-7	5.15	26	25	0	0	1	1	148.2	180	89	85	22	2	35	0	81	1	0	.301
MEMPHIS	0-0	3.00	1	1	0	0	1	0	6	6	2	2	0	0	1	0	5	0	0	.261
MAJORS																				
9 YEARS	72-67	4.55	253	184	9	3	32	2	1,242.1	1,323	662	628	151	40	388	22	799	34	2	.274

5

★20 09★

Pujols

FIRST BASEMAN

HEIGHT: 6-FOOT-3
BATS: RIGHT   THROWS: RIGHT
BIRTHDATE: JAN. 16, 1980
BIRTHPLACE: SANTO DOMINGO, D.R.

2008	AVG	G	AB	R	H	2B	3B	HR	RBI	SH	SF	HBP	BB	IBB	SO	SB	CS	GDP	SLG	OBA	E
ST. LOUIS	.357	148	524	100	187	44	0	37	116	0	8	5	104	34	54	7	3	16	.653	.462	6
MAJORS																					
8 YEARS	.334	1,239	4,578	947	1,531	342	13	319	977	1	47	60	696	154	506	45	26	157	.624	.425	79

28

★20 09★

Rasmus

OUTFIELDER

HEIGHT: 6-FOOT-2
BATS: LEFT   THROWS: LEFT
BIRTHDATE: AUG. 11, 1986
BIRTHPLACE: COLUMBUS, GA.

2008	AVG	G	AB	R	H	2B	3B	HR	RBI	SH	SF	HBP	BB	IBB	SO	SB	CS	GDP	SLG	OBA	E
MEMPHIS	.251	90	331	56	83	15	0	11	36	3	3	1	49	3	72	15	3	7	.396	.346	4
GCL CARDS	.556	3	9	1	5	1	0	1	2	0	0	0	3	0	2	0	0	0	1.000	.667	0
PALM BEACH	.000	3	9	1	0	0	0	0	0	0	0	1	1	0	3	0	0	0	.000	.182	0
MINORS 4 YEARS	.277	417	1,533	269	425	95	16	64	222	7	13	23	200	10	348	74	17	14	.485	.366	24

★20 09★

Reyes

RELIEF PITCHER

HEIGHT: 6-FOOT-3
BATS: RIGHT   THROWS: LEFT
BIRTHDATE: APRIL 19, 1977
BIRTHPLACE: HIGUERA DE
ZARAGOZA, MEXICO

2008	W-L	ERA	G	GS	CG	SHO	GF	SV	IP	H	R	ER	HR	HBP	BB	IBB	SO	WP	BK	BAA
MINNESOTA	3-0	2.33	75	0	0	0	16	0	46.1	40	12	12	4	2	15	2	39	5	0	.235
MAJORS																				
12 YEARS	32-32	4.28	535	40	0	0	97	2	646	653	349	307	57	16	356	25	583	61	7	.266

13

★ 20   09 ★

Ryan

INFIELDER

HEIGHT: 6-FOOT-2
BATS: RIGHT   THROWS: RIGHT
BIRTHDATE: MARCH 26, 1982
BIRTHPLACE: LOS ANGELES, CALIF.

2008	AVG	G	AB	R	H	2B	3B	HR	RBI	SH	SF	HBP	BB	IBB	SO	SB	CS	GDP	SLG	OBA	E
ST. LOUIS	.244	80	197	30	48	9	0	0	10	3	0	2	16	0	31	7	2	4	.289	.307	3
PALM BEACH	.250	3	12	1	3	1	0	0	0	0	0	0	1	0	1	1	1	0	.333	.308	1
SPRINGFIELD	.368	4	19	5	7	3	0	1	3	0	0	1	1	0	6	1	0	0	.684	.429	0
MEMPHIS	.221	20	77	11	17	5	0	3	8	2	1	1	4	0	17	1	0	0	.413	.279	0
MAJORS																					
2 YEARS	.265	147	377	60	100	18	0	4	22	6	0	3	31	0	50	14	2	7	.345	.326	13

55

Schumaker

SECOND BASEMAN/OUTFIELDER

HEIGHT: 5-FOOT-10
BATS: LEFT   THROWS: RIGHT
BIRTHDATE: FEB. 3, 1980
BIRTHPLACE: TORRANCE, CALIF.

2008	AVG	G	AB	R	H	2B	3B	HR	RBI	SH	SF	HBP	BB	IBB	SO	SB	CS	GDP	SLG	OBA	E
ST. LOUIS	.302	153	540	87	163	22	5	8	46	4	1	2	47	2	60	8	2	19	.406	.359	3
MAJORS																					
4 YEARS	.299	296	795	118	238	36	7	11	68	6	3	2	62	3	88	12	4	25	.404	.350	5

19

★20 09★
Stavinoha

OUTFIELDER

HEIGHT: 6-FOOT-2
BATS: RIGHT   THROWS: RIGHT
BIRTHDATE: MAY 3, 1982
BIRTHPLACE: HOUSTON, TEXAS

2008	AVG	G	AB	R	H	2B	3B	HR	RBI	SH	SF	HBP	BB	IBB	SO	SB	CS	GDP	SLG	OBA	E
MEMPHIS	.337	112	427	67	144	23	3	16	74	0	4	2	20	0	50	2	1	12	.518	.366	2
ST. LOUIS	.193	29	57	4	11	1	0	0	4	1	1	0	2	1	11	0	0	2	.211	.217	0
MAJORS																					
1 YEAR	.193	29	57	4	11	1	0	0	4	1	1	0	2	1	11	0	0	2	.211	.217	0

48

★20   09★

Thompson

RELIEF PITCHER

HEIGHT: 6-FOOT-1
BATS: RIGHT   THROWS: RIGHT
BIRTHDATE: JAN. 31, 1982
BIRTHPLACE: LAS VEGAS, NEV.

2008	W-L	ERA	G	GS	CG	SHO	GF	SV	IP	H	R	ER	HR	HBP	BB	IBB	SO	WP	BK	BAA
ST. LOUIS	6-3	5.15	26	6	0	0	10	0	64.2	72	38	37	5	3	19	1	32	2	0	.293
MEMPHIS	1-1	7.82	3	3	0	0	0	0	12.1	22	13	11	4	0	2	0	4	0	0	.367
MAJORS																				
4 YEARS	19-11	4.24	153	24	0	0	44	1	305.2	333	159	144	37	25	94	8	146	7	0	.281

★ 20   09 ★

Thurston

INFIELDER

HEIGHT: 5-FOOT-11
BATS: LEFT   THROWS: RIGHT
BIRTHDATE: SEPT. 29, 1979
BIRTHPLACE: FAIRFIELD, CALIF.

2008	AVG	G	AB	R	H	2B	3B	HR	RBI	SH	SF	HBP	BB	IBB	SO	SB	CS	GDP	SLG	OBA	E
PAWTUCKET	.316	126	507	84	160	28	5	11	64	14	8	11	35	1	75	19	11	8	.456	.367	9
BOSTON	.000	4	8	0	0	0	0	0	0	0	0	1	0	0	1	0	0	0	.000	.111	0
MAJORS																					
5 YEARS	.227	59	66	7	15	3	1	0	2	1	2	2	2	0	10	0	0	0	.303	.264	1

50

ADAM WAINW... WAINWRIGHT

★ 20 09 ★

Wainwright

STARTING PITCHER

HEIGHT: 6-FOOT-7
BATS: RIGHT   THROWS: RIGHT
BIRTHDATE: AUG. 30, 1981
BIRTHPLACE: BRUNSWICK, GA.

2008	W-L	ERA	G	GS	CG	SHO	GF	SV	IP	H	R	ER	HR	HBP	BB	IBB	SO	WP	BK	BAA
ST. LOUIS	11-3	3.20	20	20	1	0	0	0	132	122	51	47	12	3	34	1	91	3	0	.245
MEMPHIS	0-1	12.27	2	2	0	0	0	0	3.2	8	5	5	1	0	1	0	3	0	0	.444
SPRINGFIELD	0-0	0.00	1	1	0	0	0	0	4.2	4	0	0	0	0	0	0	7	0	0	.222
MAJORS 4 YEARS	27-16	3.48	115	52	2	0	11	3	411	400	173	159	32	16	127	7	299	12	0	.254

37

★ 20 09 ★

Wellemeyer

STARTING PITCHER

HEIGHT: 6-FOOT-3
BATS: RIGHT   THROWS: RIGHT
BIRTHDATE: AUG. 30, 1978
BIRTHPLACE: LOUISVILLE, KY.

2008	W-L	ERA	G	GS	CG	SHO	GF	SV	IP	H	R	ER	HR	HBP	BB	IBB	SO	WP	BK	BAA
ST. LOUIS	13-9	3.71	32	32	0	0	0	0	191.2	178	84	79	25	7	62	1	134	7	1	.245
MAJORS																				
6 YEARS	22-19	4.42	167	43	0	0	38	3	433.2	407	233	213	55	14	213	10	340	23	2	.250

★20 09★

Mitchell Boggs

PITCHER -41-

HEIGHT: 6-FOOT-4 BATS: RIGHT
THROWS: RIGHT BIRTHDATE: FEB. 15, 1984
BIRTHPLACE: DALTON, GA.

2008	W-L	ERA	G	GS	CG	SHO	GF	SV	IP	H	R	ER	HR	HBP	BB	IBB	SO	WP	BK	BAA
ST. LOUIS	3-2	7.41	8	6	0	0	1	0	34	42	29	28	5	2	22	0	13	2	0	.304
MEMPHIS	9-3	3.45	21	21	1	0	0	0	125.1	107	52	48	11	2	46	0	81	10	1	.235
MAJORS																				
1 YEAR	3-2	7.41	8	6	0	0	1	0	34	42	29	28	5	2	22	0	13	2	0	.304

★20 09★

David Freese

THIRD BASEMAN -12-

HEIGHT: 6-FOOT-2 BATS: RIGHT
THROWS: RIGHT BIRTHDATE: APRIL 28, 1983
BIRTHPLACE: CORPUS CHRISTI, TEXAS

2008	AVG	G	AB	R	H	2B	3B	HR	RBI	SH	SF	HBP	BB	IBB	SO	SB	CS	GDP	SLG	OBA	E
MEMPHIS	.306	131	464	83	142	29	3	26	91	0	4	3	39	0	111	5	2	11	.550	.361	10
MINORS																					
3 YEARS	.307	330	1,229	233	377	81	12	56	257	0	11	27	136	1	266	12	4	26	.529	.385	30

★20 09★

Troy Glaus

THIRD BASEMAN -8-

HEIGHT: 6-FOOT-5 BATS: RIGHT
THROWS: RIGHT BIRTHDATE: AUG. 3, 1976
BIRTHPLACE: TARZANA, CALIF.

2008	AVG	G	AB	R	H	2B	3B	HR	RBI	SH	SF	HBP	BB	IBB	SO	SB	CS	GDP	SLG	OBA	E
ST. LOUIS	.270	151	544	69	147	33	1	27	99	0	3	3	87	3	104	0	1	14	.483	.372	7
MAJORS																					
11 YEARS	.256	1,395	4,969	835	1,271	273	10	304	877	0	41	42	788	38	1,269	56	29	121	.498	.360	170

Blake Hawksworth

RELIEF PITCHER -53-

HEIGHT: 6-FOOT-3 BATS: RIGHT
THROWS: RIGHT BIRTHDATE: MARCH 1, 1983
BIRTHPLACE: NORTH VANCOUVER, B.C.

2008	W-L	ERA	G	GS	CG	SHO	GF	SV	IP	H	R	ER	HR	HBP	BB	IBB	SO	WP	BK	BAA
MEMPHIS	5-7	6.09	18	16	0	0	0	0	88.2	111	71	60	12	8	38	1	83	7	1	.307
GCL CARDS	0-0	0.00	2	2	0	0	0	0	7	2	0	0	0	0	2	0	6	0	0	.091
MINORS																				
7 YEARS	30-35	4.06	112	108	0	0	0	0	576.1	567	296	260	56	37	187	1	479	36	6	.260

Josh Kinney

RELIEF PITCHER -52-

HEIGHT: 6-FOOT-1 BATS: RIGHT
THROWS: RIGHT BIRTHDATE: MARCH 31, 1979
BIRTHPLACE: COUDERSPORT, PA.

2008	W-L	ERA	G	GS	CG	SHO	GF	SV	IP	H	R	ER	HR	HBP	BB	IBB	SO	WP	BK	BAA
SPRINGFIELD	0-1	7.36	4	0	0	0	0	0	3.2	4	3	3	0	1	0	0	5	0	0	.286
ST. LOUIS	0-0	0.00	7	0	0	0	1	0	7	3	0	0	0	0	1	0	8	0	0	.125
MAJORS																				
2 YEARS	0-0	2.53	28	0	0	0	5	0	32	20	9	9	3	1	9	0	30	0	0	.175

Joe Mather

OUTFIELDER/THIRD BASEMAN -7-

HEIGHT: 6-FOOT-4 BATS: RIGHT
THROWS: RIGHT BIRTHDATE: JULY 23, 1982
BIRTHPLACE: SANDPOINT, IDAHO

2008	AVG	G	AB	R	H	2B	3B	HR	RBI	SH	SF	HBP	BB	IBB	SO	SB	CS	GDP	SLG	OBA	E
MEMPHIS	.303	59	211	45	64	14	2	17	41	1	2	8	32	0	36	7	2	6	.630	.411	3
ST. LOUIS	.241	54	133	20	32	7	0	8	18	0	1	1	12	1	32	1	0	2	.474	.306	1
MAJORS																					
1 YEAR	.241	54	133	20	32	7	0	8	18	0	1	1	12	1	32	1	0	2	.474	.306	1

Shane Robinson

OUTFIELDER -33-

HEIGHT: 5-FOOT-9   BATS: RIGHT
THROWS: RIGHT   BIRTHDATE: OCT. 30, 1984
BIRTHPLACE: TAMPA, FLA.

2008	AVG	G	AB	R	H	2B	3B	HR	RBI	SH	SF	HBP	BB	IBB	SO	SB	CS	GDP	SLG	OBA	E
SPRINGFIELD	.352	63	244	46	86	17	3	4	32	3	4	3	17	0	34	13	5	4	.496	.396	2
MEMPHIS	.220	42	141	10	31	4	1	1	10	2	2	1	5	0	24	2	3	3	.284	.248	0
MINORS	.285	215	814	120	232	36	7	8	77	9	12	12	60	1	95	42	15	20	.376	.339	5

Jess Todd

RELIEF PITCHER -30-

HEIGHT: 5-FOOT-11   BATS: RIGHT
THROWS: RIGHT   BIRTHDATE: APRIL 20, 1986
BIRTHPLACE: LONGVIEW, TEXAS

2008	W-L	ERA	G	GS	CG	SHO	GF	SV	IP	H	R	ER	HR	HBP	BB	IBB	SO	WP	BK	BAA
PALM BEACH	3-0	1.65	7	4	0	0	1	1	27.1	18	7	5	0	1	7	0	35	0	1	.184
SPRINGFIELD	4-5	2.97	17	16	0	0	1	0	103	79	37	34	12	13	24	1	81	1	0	.216
MEMPHIS	1-1	3.97	4	4	0	0	0	0	22.2	19	10	10	4	1	11	0	20	2	0	.232
MINORS	12-7	2.85	44	31	0	0	4	1	211.1	164	77	67	18	16	56	2	205	5	1	.216

P.J. Walters

RELIEF PITCHER -62-

HEIGHT: 6-FOOT-4   BATS: RIGHT
THROWS: RIGHT   BIRTHDATE: MARCH 12, 1985
BIRTHPLACE: DOTHAN, ALA.

2008	W-L	ERA	G	GS	CG	SHO	GF	SV	IP	H	R	ER	HR	HBP	BB	IBB	SO	WP	BK	BAA
SPRINGFIELD	1-2	3.25	6	6	0	0	0	0	36	35	17	13	5	3	8	0	34	2	0	.252
MEMPHIS	9-4	4.87	23	23	0	0	0	0	122	123	71	66	17	8	62	2	122	11	1	.266
MINORS 3 YEARS	24-13	3.55	85	52	1	0	23	9	340	317	151	134	31	27	112	2	334	23	1	.245

MEMPHIS REDBIRDS
Pacific Coast League, Class AAA

MANAGER: CHRIS MALONEY
COACHES: MARK BUDASKA (BATTING), BLAISE ILSLEY (PITCHING)
CARDINALS AFFILIATE SINCE: 1998
LENGTH OF SEASON: 144 GAMES (APRIL 9 - SEPT. 7)
BALLPARK: AUTOZONE PARK (14,384 CAPACITY)
DIMENSIONS: LF: 319 • LCF: 360 • CF: 400 • RCF: 373 • RF: 322
ADDRESS: 175 TOYOTA PLAZA #300, MEMPHIS, TN 38103
PHONE: 901-721-6050
WEB SITE: MEMPHISREDBIRDS.COM

SPRINGFIELD CARDINALS
Texas League, Class AA

MANAGER: RON "POP" WARNER
COACHES: DERRICK MAY (BATTING), BRYAN EVERSGERD (PITCHING)
CARDINALS AFFILIATE SINCE: 2005
LENGTH OF SEASON: 140 GAMES, SPLIT HALF-SEASONS
(APRIL 9 – SEPT. 7)
BALLPARK: HAMMONS FIELD (6,750 CAPACITY)
DIMENSIONS: LF: 315 • LCF: 365 • CF: 400 • RCF: 365 • RF: 330
ADDRESS: 955 EAST TRAFFICWAY, SPRINGFIELD, MO 65802
PHONE: 417-863-0395
WEB SITE: SPRINGFIELDCARDINALS.COM

PALM BEACH CARDINALS
Florida State League, Class A Advanced

MANAGER: TOM SPENCER
COACHES: JEFF ALBERT (BATTING), DENNIS MARTINEZ (PITCHING)
CARDINALS AFFILIATE SINCE: 2003
LENGTH OF SEASON: 140 GAMES, SPLIT HALF-SEASONS
(APRIL 9 – SEPT. 6)
BALLPARK: ROGER DEAN STADIUM (6,871 CAPACITY)
DIMENSIONS: LF: 335 • LCF: 380 • CF: 400 • RCF: 375 • RF: 325
ADDRESS: 4751 MAIN ST., JUPITER, FL 33458
PHONE: 561-775-1818
WEB SITE: PALMBEACHCARDINALS.COM

QUAD CITIES RIVER BANDITS
Midwest League, Class A

MANAGER: STEVE DILLARD
COACHES: JOE KRUZEL (BATTING), ARTHUR "ACE" ADAMS (PITCHING)
CARDINALS AFFILIATE SINCE: 2005
LENGTH OF SEASON: 140 GAMES, SPLIT HALF-SEASONS
(APRIL 9 – SEPT. 7)
BALLPARK: MODERN WOODMEN PARK (6,300 CAPACITY)
DIMENSIONS: LF: 343 • LCF: 383 • CF: 400 • RCF: 370 • RF: 318
ADDRESS: 209 S. GAINES ST., DAVENPORT, IA 52802
PHONE: 563-322-6348
WEB SITE: RIVERBANDITS.COM

BATAVIA MUCKDOGS
New York-Penn League, Short-Season Class A

MANAGER: MARK DeJOHN
COACHES: RAMON ORTIZ (BATTING), TIM LEVEQUE (PITCHING)
CARDINALS AFFILIATE SINCE: 2007
LENGTH OF SEASON: 76 GAMES (JUNE 19 – SEPT. 6)
BALLPARK: DWYER STADIUM (2,600 CAPACITY)
DIMENSIONS: LF: 325 • LCF: 354 • CF: 400 • RCF: 354 • RF: 325
ADDRESS: 299 BANK ST., BATAVIA, NY 14020
PHONE: 585-343-5454
WEB SITE: MUCKDOGS.COM

JOHNSON CITY CARDINALS
Appalachian League, Rookie

MANAGER: MIKE SHILDT
COACHES: JOHNNY RODRIGUEZ (BATTING), DOUG WHITE
(PITCHING)
CARDINALS AFFILIATE SINCE: 1975
LENGTH OF SEASON: 68 GAMES (JUNE 23 – SEPT. 1)
BALLPARK: HOWARD JOHNSON FIELD (2,500 CAPACITY)
DIMENSIONS: LF: 320 • CF: 410 • RF: 320
ADDRESS: 111 LEGION ST., JOHNSON CITY, TN 37601
PHONE: 423-461-4866
WEB SITE: JCCARDINALS.COM

Gulf Coast League

GULF COAST CARDINALS
Gulf Coast League, Rookie

MANAGER: STEVE TURCO
COACHES: NEDER HORTA (BATTING), DERNIER OROZCO (PITCHING)
CARDINALS AFFILIATE SINCE: 2007
LENGTH OF SEASON: 56 GAMES, SPLIT HALF-SEASONS
(JUNE 23 – AUG. 21)
BALLPARK: CARDINALS COMPLEX, FIELD NO. 1
DIMENSIONS: LF: 319 • LCF: 360 • CF: 400 • RCF: 373 • RF: 322
ADDRESS: 4751 MAIN ST., JUPITER, FL 33458
PHONE: 561-775-1818

Dominican Summer League

DOMINICAN CARDINALS
Dominican Summer League, Rookie

MANAGER: CLAUDIO ALMONTE
COACHES: RENE ROJAS (BATTING), BILL VILLANUEVA (PITCHING)
CARDINALS AFFILIATE SINCE: 2005
LENGTH OF SEASON: 72 GAMES (MAY 30 - AUG. 21)
BALLPARK: ACADEMIA DE BASEBALL CARDENALES DE SAN LUIS

Venezuelan Summer League

VENEZUELAN CARDINALS
Venezuelan Summer League, Rookie

MANAGER: ENRIQUE BRITO
COACHES: JESUS LAYA (BATTING), HENDERSON LUGO (PITCHING)
CARDINALS AFFILIATE SINCE: 2006
LENGTH OF SEASON: 64 GAMES (MAY 18 – AUG. 8)

1966 National League All-Stars

Allied Photos
20, 32-33, 42, 43, 44, 52, 53, 54, 63, 81, 82, 86, 88, 99, 102, 110, 116, 117 bottom, 191

Arteaga Photos
96, 108

Dan Donovan/St. Louis Cardinals
132, 134, 136, 140, 142, 146, 148, 150, 154, 156, 158, 160, 162, 164, 166, 168, 170, 172, 174, 176, 178

Getty Images
46, 90 left, 105, 111, 114, 121, 122, 125, 126, 128 top, 185, 186, 187 middle and bottom, 131, 133, 135, 137, 141, 143, 145, 147, 149, 151, 153, 155, 157, 159, 161, 163, 165, 167, 171, 173, 175, 177, 179, 181, 183

Bill Greenblatt/UPI
144, 182

Jim Herren/St. Louis Cardinals
187 top

Scott Rovak/St. Louis Cardinals
138, 139, 152, 169, 180

St. Louis Mercantile Library/Globe-Democrat Collection
12, 13 right, 18-19, 29, 35 bottom, 37 top, 41, 47, 48, 49, 60-61, 65, 70, 72, 74-75, 77, 78, 80, 89, 90-91 middle, 91 right, 92, 93 bottom, 94, 98, 103

Herb Scharfman/Sports Illustrated/Getty Images
120

Sporting News
14, 15, 16, 21, 25, 26, 34, 36, 37 bottom, 58, 59, 62, 64, 71, 76, 93 top, 104

All other photos from Cardinals Archives

We've parked you close.
We've got you covered.
Now, we've made it easy.

Stadium East and Stadium West have always provided the closest covered parking to Busch Stadium. The 2009 Preferred Parking Program gives you even more!

For more information, visit us on the web:
www.interparkonline.com/cardinalparking
or call 314.421.2613.

InterPark